HOW TO PLAN A

SPECTACULAR

FAMILY REUNION

HOW TO PLAN A

Spectacular

FAMILY REUNION -

DISCOVERING RELATIONSHIPS

**From Picnics and Talent Shows To Oral
Histories and Family Themes
Genealogy and Family Inve$tment$**

Geneva Turner, PhD, RN, CFLE

*A Family Projects Book / TACF
Columbus, GA*

Published by:
Family Projects Publishers/TACF
Columbus, Georgia 1993

Library of Congress Catalog Card Number 92-97520
ISBN 1-882977-00-9

Printed in the United States of America

Publisher's Cataloging in Publication Data
Turner, Geneva
  How To Plan A Spectacular Family Reunion-Discovering Relationships: From Picnics
  and Talent Shows To Oral Histories and Family Themes, Genealogy and Family
  Inve$tment$
Geneva Turner.
Bibliography
Includes Index
1. Planning family reunions
2. Family meals
3. Family activities
4. Oral histories
5. Written family histories
6. Family themes
7. Genealogy
8. Family investments
ISBN 1-882977-00-9: $12.95 Softcover

No rose without a thorn
English Proverb, XV Century

"A family
is like a
beautiful rose!
Each part is unique and
essential. Petals - delicate and
beautiful. Stem - strong and
sturdy. Leaves - nurturing
and vibrant. Thorns -
protective and enigmatic.
Petals,
stem,
leaves and
thorns are
intricately arranged
by nature to
produce a
flower
of
aesthetic
quality
with
beauty
that
is
enhanced
by each
part-
even
its
thorns."

Geneva Turner

This book is dedicated in memory of my father,
George Robert Turner and in honor of my mother,
Mollie Bell Nelson Turner, and to the rest of my family,
a diverse group of people in all shapes and sizes,
geographic locations, ways of viewing the world and of interpreting
symbols. My family - individuals who are creative, intelligent,
industrious, and honest with similarities that bind and link
differences and commonalities. My family, a true example of a
thorned rose.

The author has not made an attempt, by publishing this book, to indicate that activities or suggestions will work for each and every family. The success of your reunion depends on organization and family attitudes.

The purpose of this book is to serve as a guide for readers in planning a family reunion. The author simply encourages everyone to utilize a reunion as an opportunity to connect with your family's past and to discover relationships.

Please seek accounting, legal, and tax counsel before implementing any important investment ideas. Information included is general information only and not a substitute for more specific advice.

ACKNOWLEDGEMENTS

The influence of numerous persons deserve recognition, some are deceased and others are very much alive. By experiencing life with them, I have been inspired to excel. Most of these persons are family members, others exist in their own family circles. All have inspired me because of the love they demonstrate each and every day for their relatives.

A special thank you is given to Connie Turner, chair of the first Turner/Jones Family Reunion and to succeeding chairpersons: Freddie Buckley, Henry Turner and Emma Moore. A nod of respect goes to Area Coordinators who work diligently to ensure that I do not crumble as the chairperson for 1993, Henry Turner, Denver, Colorado; Freddie Buckley, Melvindale, Michigan; Charlie Turner, Ecorse, Michigan; Emma Moore, Orlando, Florida; Alice T. Burch, Radcliff, Kentucky; Milton Turner, Montgomery, Alabama; Nettie Leonard, Yvette Turner Lackland and Robert Leonard, Columbus, Georgia; Dorothy Hurd, Bessemer, Alabama; Neal Jones, Newark, New Jersey; Dolores Mackey, Philadelphia, Pennsylvania; Ernestine Dill, Catonsville, MD; and Melvin Turner, Gary, Indiana.

Cheers to cousins Robert Leonard of Econoprint, Columbus, Georgia and Norma Paige of Paige II Image Enhancers, Denver, Colorado for designing and donating stationery for our reunions.

Kudos to Alice Burch and W. Curtis Stephens for reviewing this manuscript.

Mountains of gratitude to Uncles Henry and Thomas Turner who expressed a universal truism - *meeting at funerals has to end.*
To George Robert and Mollie Turner for years of demonstrating that a positive family life makes all the difference in a child's success. And to my Aunt Willie Pitts Turner *who always knew.*

PRAISES TO EACH OF YOU!

Table of Contents

Part III: Investing In Your Family's Future

Part IV: Putting It All Together

PREFACE

In 1976 in Nurnberg, Germany a haze of brown and white jacketed books titled *Roots* were supported under arms and rested in hands of personnel at the United States Army Hospital. Being an avid reader, when I found this mysterious book in the military bookstore, I, too, became its victim. I could not put it down until I had read every page.

As I became a part of the very graphic description of past life put to words by Alex Haley, my mind flashed on numerous trips to "the country" to visit relatives. That year, I vowed to discover relationships among family members and connect with past life in both parents' family lines.

Years have passed since experiencing vicarious exploration of family history and of remembering visits with relatives. These vivid memories serve as the impetus for this book - discovering relationships through connection with the past by way of family reunions.

P
R
O
L
O
G
U
E

The Beginning

Each person's childhood carries with it treasured memories. Mine is no exception. I remember my father navigating through miles and miles of unpaved roads in a maze with no houses in sight. I also remember being fascinated by the great mental effort it must caused for him to find his relatives with, what seemed to me then, no land marks.

Our days began much too early in the morning and some trips started after church on Sunday, and ended much too late at night. My father packed a lunch while my mother made sure each of us (sometimes six and most of the time nine siblings) were properly dressed for our visits. We piled into our car, and, years later, into a very much needed green and white station wagon on a 80 or 100 mile journey that seemed to take hours.

My oldest brother and sister were in college so they escaped many of these visits. As I grew older, and like my siblings before me, I found excuses for not accompanying my parents on each and every trip. I enjoyed meeting and visiting relatives. However, it seemed as though my father would get stuck in a time warp and had difficulty returning to the present decade. I wanted to end our visit early and return to bright lights and noise. This leap of faith would have ended our visit among the crickets, frogs, cows and vegetables.

Today, retrieval of valuable family history is difficult; most who experienced it are deceased. When I was a child, history was in the making. During our visits, adults talked non-stop as children only partially listened, and sometimes not at all, when the urge to play hit us.

Now that I am older, my siblings and I appreciate those visits back in time and our parents' patience in sharing what they knew of our family histories. My father is deceased, if he were alive today, he would stand atop a box and exclaim, *I told you so.*

He was right about most aspects in life (especially, about buying American), two concern this book: the family and reunions. So many years and reunions later, with my father's philosophy in mind, this book, or manual as I often speak of it, was designed to assist you to visit with your relatives in a

SPECTACULAR way. Another *Roots* it is not. However, it is a how-to manual with activities that decrease the work of a reunion for a committee or chairperson.

Today, more and more families plan family gatherings. And with good reason. The 60s heralded the days of free sex, the mood of those days continued into the 70s. In the 80s, Americans focused on "I and me." The 90s predict a commitment to values, family relations, and building family strength - a welcomed change.

By purchasing this manual, you're in tune with scientific predictions. Also, you must have a reunion to plan or you think it is about time your family connected. Believe me, the first gathering will require a great deal of energy. *Wait awhile though* before you change your mind about this project. Please realize that like vintage wine, reunions do get better.

Change is inevitable for the environment and for people. A reunion brings individuals together to celebrate similarities and to reflect on history that determined their existence before everybody "grew up" and somehow *changed.*

Most people in our highly mobile and technical society are racing at a fast pace to earn a living and keep track of an immediate family whose members have diverse hobbies and occupations that carry them miles from home on any given day. Keeping up with extended family members, sometimes, becomes low priority as schedules are kept.

As you will discover, and most probably already know, a family reunion can be as creative as your family will allow. A typical reunion, for relatives living in close proximity to one another, consists of a half day of activities proximity to one another, consists of a half day of activities one or more times a year. Some people believe that this time, eight or more hours, is *just about enough time to linger in the past with people they don't really know.* If family members are really spread apart, traveling hundreds or thousands of miles for eight hours just is not feasible. If your family fits this group of reunioners, a longer time together is more logical.

Whatever amount of time you choose, a family reunion is *the best way* to continue family ties and to discover relationships. Whether you have planned several or if you are planning your first, you will eventually realize that all of the hard work was worth the fun you will have and the relationships you will discover. So read on, its time to get busy!

MANUAL PREPARATION

No attempt has been made to present information on family theory or family dynamics. Other resources are available for that purpose. However, the information here is written to serve as a practical guide for anyone interested in connecting with their family history and in discovering relationships among existing family members.

This manual/book is divided into four sections or parts. Part I focuses on reunion activities and organization; Part II describes genealogy and gathering information from your family and other sources; Part III relates ideas for investing in your family's financial future, also, points are included for continuing closeness; and, finally, Part IV gives a description of approaches for novice and experienced reunion organizers when it is time to put it all together.

Each chapter includes important points that are chapter highlights and pages for notes.

Chapter One: Discovering Relationships
Many topics are discussed including classification of reunion attendees that range from *Fun-loving to Combination.*

Chapter Two: *Organizing Your Reunion*
Detailed informal and formal reunion organization strategies

Chapter Three: *Let Us Break Bread Together: Count The Many Ways*
Eleven ways to serve food to your relatives and tips for each are presented

Chapter Four: *Planning A Get Acquainted Session*
This chapter includes tips for getting to know all relatives during initial contact

Chapter Five: *Tours and Other Outdoor Activities*
Tours, tours, and more tours. This chapter also provides information for *free time*

Chapter Six: *Special Activities*
These activities include a proclamation, key to the city, newspaper article, fun run/walk, many others

Chapter Seven: Especially *For Kids*
Fun games for your family's youth and how to include them as co-organizers

Chapter Eight: Organizing Your Investigation
Provides information for the person gathering a
family history

Chapter Nine: *Getting Information*
Tips to ensure that investigation of family history is
successful

Chapter Ten: *Genealogy*
A description of genealogy and how to access
family information from non-family sources

Chapter Eleven: *Your Family's Future*
Ways to stimulate your family's financial future

Chapter Twelve: *Continuing The Closeness*
Includes interesting ways to enhance togetherness

Chapter Thirteen: *Putting It All Together*
Summarizes other chapters, shows how
previous information enhances a reunion.

Appendices include examples of forms and essential
ideas that enhance any family reunion.

-Lets begin-

PART I
Reunion Activities

CHAPTER

ONE:

Discovering Relationships

As you read through this book, it becomes apparent that two words are used quite often: derivatives of *discover* and *connect*. Both terms are quite appropriate. When families get together for extended periods of time, connections are made when newly discovered relatives become a part of the family's inner circle. Reunions afford families with opportunities to draw all relations together and to strengthen as a unit.

DISCOVERY BEGINS

The immense talent and similar philosophies in your family will surprise you. People you knew existed but had limited or no contact prior to the reunion are, you will discover, a lot like you.

In today's society, we are faced with numerous obstacles that beset well intentioned plans: economy and unemployment. These problems and others are just a few that are solved through family unity. Anytime twenty or more people are in a room, experts on many topics surface. The same exists with your family - undiscovered experts.

What does knowing about your family members' specialties have to do with a family reunion? A great deal. There is no better way to get assistance if you are stagnated or if a problem exists. Even better, why not honor someone during a reunion for excelling in their field?

Here is a preview of activities included in the remaining pages of this book. Create your own *award system*. A Pulitzer Prize and an Academy Award are both treasured awards. Your family's award can hold similar esteem for your relatives. The intent is to present an award to someone who does something extra. Give the award with love and respect. Develop specific and stringent guidelines and applaud each other.

Another idea, lets suppose for a brief moment that no one in your family has problems. Each relative is a high achiever. Design a program, have known family experts address ways to prevent problems with the economy, unemployment and other topics.

How many times have you needed assistance from an expert and someone mentions that a distant relative has years of experience on that very topic. Lets suppose you could even pay that relative for their services. Wouldn't it be better to get advice from a family member than to go to a stranger? In many cases, when you seek counsel of your relative, a bond of friendship is made. This is an excellent way to improve the economic standing within your family, instead of giving your money to a non-relative.

How can you find out about your relatives' occupations? You ask them. It is just that simple. Explain what you are going to do. Here is another idea. Compile a *family reference guide* with occupations, hobbies, birthdates, children, areas of expertise, addresses and telephone numbers. You will discover that this kind of guide is more useful than recording addresses and telephone numbers only.

FAMILY ISOLATION

Every family has experienced painful situations caused by family members or by other persons. Some of those experiences have lasting effects; others produce family feuds, splits, dissolution and dysfunction.

Now that you are planning a reunion, what are you to do with those relatives? Do you invite them? Or are you expected to continue to foster your family's self-instituted policing? Appropriate responses to these questions do not exist for each and every situation. If you are in this position, tread lightly as you make decisions.

But who has decided to be judge and jury in a situation that occurred long ago. Maybe a relative did not pay a debt, caused someone to lose a political race, shared a family secret. If you were not a witness to the situation, you are at a greater disadvantage. Do you want to be a party to the overblown battle? Or is it time to put all of this aside?

The accused person probably wants to get on with life. And if your relatives are licking wounds that were injured years ago, believe me, there is no way anyone can get on with life. Past events that carry negative energy should not occupy all of their attention or require anyone's best energy.

You know your family, and you are aware of the situation that occurred. Lets suppose that years ago, decades before you were conceived, you heard that a very young Aunt *DROPPED* a baby. You found out that the alienated Aunt was a minor when the accident occurred. However, because of accepted practices during that period in history, children her age were required to assume adult roles. What are you to do? Maybe it *was* an accident. If the person's descendants receive invitations, and come, what will other relatives do?

Now, there is another step to this situation. Who is going to extend the white flag? A reunion makes it all possible.

LONELINESS

For some, this situation is short of being isolated. Bringing familiar faces together during a reunion is a way to decrease loneliness. Relatives are reacquainted and often communication continues until the next reunion.

As individuals focus on self actualization and self discovery, change will occur. To discover who you are and what you can do requires a lot of positive energy toward those goals. People who have experienced that level of life and others who have no concept of it, unfortunately, will have strained relationships. Sometimes, this situation occurs in families and distancing sets in.

Families are often in various stages of transition. In addition, family members experience varying developmental levels simultaneously. Needs differ and social contacts vary. Regardless of the agenda, participation in family rituals should be respected as schedules permit.

In this country, as we forge ahead daily seeking the American dream, we should not loose sight of immediate treasures that offer immeasurable wealth, family ties. Many have and will discover that *to obtain financial security at the expense of ones family is to prosper as an emotional pauper when wealth has been attained.*

TYPES OF REUNION ATTENDEES

An unknown author wrote, "It takes all kinds to make a family." I can assure you that this anonymous quotation will prove to be true for your reunion attendees. All personality types will attend. Your relatives probably fit descriptions below (WARNING: THIS INFORMATION IS INCLUDED AS LIGHTHEARTED ENTERTAINMENT): fun-loving, just folks, braggots, skeptics (this group will outweigh the rest at first), angry ones, and two groups that exist in every family - own world and combination. An examination of each will provide any planner/organizer/chairperson with an idea of activities to plan and opportunities for laughter.

Fun-loving

When the invitation is received, if fun is included, this group will be there. Count on them. If the reunion hits an all time low, this group will make their own fun even before the low sets in. About 50% of your family members are fun-loving people, but in varying degrees. *On this group, you can depend, most of them will attend.*

Just Folks

Here is a category of kind people. They aim to please. Whatever you say is okay, they just want things to go right. Just folks are mannerable and find it difficult to say anything derogatory about anyone. They love their family, and always want to be around.

Twenty-five percent of every family consists of people who could fit this category. You can count on 50% of this group to attend. The other 50% will not request time off their jobs. They are equally committed to their jobs as well. This group will emerge as your last minute helpers when you need them.

Braggots

Braggot is a variation of the word brag. Now this group poses a wee problem for a frantic organizer who does not have time to give to the "I have" group. Relatives in this group will enjoy the reunion. They are convinced that they are the only ones with expertise on all topics. The reunion certainly would have turned out better had they been involved. Hold on to your patience when you see them coming, this group is really harmless.

Approximately 5% of every family (give or take a few) are BRAGGOTS. Of course, they will attend, how else will you know that they have more than you.

Skeptics

Here are your non-believers. In what you ask? That anything of merit will materialize.

Don't be so sensitive with this group. After all, they do not trust a sure thing when it stands on their heads. Its really not you, believe me, some will spread that your plans are a flop. People in this category don't trust their boss or the writing on their pay checks.

Every family has to have at least 2-3% of its members in this category. How else will the rest of us stay on our toes? We have to make them out to be liars. So chin up! All of your relatives in this group are coming, if they believe the dates you mailed, _if YOU really mailed the invitation._

Angry Ones

Here we go. This is the group to get a good nights sleep to greet. _Absolutely nothing is ever right for them._ And, why are they so angry? No one knows! It has nothing to do with you. Check their acquaintances (not many friends, they have argued them away), most of them are celebrating "Angry Ones" departure from their existence to attend the reunion.

These relatives really are pleasant people, somehow they have gotten the communication thing all screwed up. Most of your relatives in this group do not realize what they are doing or why people appear to be shocked at the end of a conversation with them.

Each and every family has one or two relatives (some have more than their quota) in this group. Count on at least one representative. How do you deal with them? Give them something special to do. They really want attention. I think.

Own World

We are winding down now. This group does not require an explanation. You know for a fact that you mailed each person an invitation. You actually saw this person with the information in their hand. Guess what? Relatives in this category will ask, "When did we start having reunions in our family? When you share that this one is your tenth; their response will be, "Oh, why wasn't I invited."

Don't be offended, just repeat the information; however, the person still does not understand. The best thing to do is to have a witness, *but NOT FROM THE ANGRY GROUP!*

Don't fret, usually there is only a handful per family (scattered). A few will call after the reunion to make reservations for the reunion that has already passed.

Combination

Where do I begin? Chameleon is a more appropriate term for this group (person). Again, their frustrations have absolutely nothing to do with you. In spite of everything, even this person will enjoy the reunion, even when their mood swings them into being classified as "Angry Ones."

There are one to two of this type in every family. However, some families have cornered the market. These are your fair weather people. Get ready for changes in the weather.

IMPORTANT POINTS:

1. *Get ready for surprises! Relatives you thought would not cooperate, become your best allies.*
2. *If you are planning your first reunion, do not be disappointed if your initial showing is small. Celebrate with whoever comes. Next year, and the year after, you will see your attendance double.*

NOTES:

_____

_____

_____

_____

_____

_____

_____

_____

_____

_____

_____

_____

_____

It is a bad plan that can't be changed.
-Publilius Syrus, *Moral Sayings*

C
H
A
P
T
E
R

TWO:

Organizing Your Reunion

You purchased this manual, so you must have a reunion to plan. Whatever your reason, organization is essential.

Have you ever wondered who was in charge of planning political conventions? Guess what, at first, planning your reunion will take on qualities of an international affair. I suppose, it all depends on the kind of reunion you plan: half-day, one-day, two-day, three-day, four-day, one week.

Regardless of the time length together, brave soul, you still must be very organized and flexible.

The way you organize for your reunion will depend on its format. Is it informal (Hey lets get together for a picnic next Sunday around 2:00 in the afternoon)? Or is it formal (planning a dinner, a talent show and other activities for numerous people who live all over the world, lets say next year)? Because it is easier, lets tackle informal organization first.

INFORMAL ORGANIZATION

For an informal reunion, formal plans must be made. This kind of reunion generally involves arrangements for a picnic or a dinner. People gather at the appointed time, enjoy the activity and leave the same day.

Questions: Who decided you would organize this activity? Who will plan the next one? Will you have assistance from someone who does not live with you? How will you know this? Who decides on the menu and the location? Better yet, who is going to pay for all of this?

Answers: For a single activity, it is practical to ask each extended family to bring a dish. You could take the cooperation a bit further and start a list of needed items and call each family unit.

Some families rotate total responsibility for a dinner or a picnic. Other family members have no responsibilities, except being on time for the occasion. Introductions are informal and conversation is spontaneous. Relatives are encouraged to sign a register at a convenient location in the hosting family's home or picnic area. The relative or family responsible for the next activity is announced.

Assignment of duties for an informal affair can be accomplished by assigning them to older siblings and skipping family units. Be creative, place names of family representatives in a hat. As names are withdrawn, they are placed on a calendar (especially if families meet often during the year).

Whether the reunion is informal or formal, a committee works well with this approach. This strategy prevents one family from being inundated with work and frustrated by organizing the reunion.

FORMAL ORGANIZATION

You *will* need assistance. A committee works best. Never try to do this project alone. If you do, your hair will turn gray and fall out.

Once you know your committee members, double check telephone numbers, addresses and correct spelling of names. Decide on a meeting date that is convenient for most members. Get several choices, you can make changes depending on your schedule.

The reunion committee is charged with arranging the absolute best occasion for your entire family. Consider all family members. As chair, you must remember that not all family members can afford to stay in an exclusive hotel in a city without reasonable rates on anything, especially food that costs the price of some utility bills.

Prepare for your committee meeting. Remember, this is a business meeting. Devise an agenda and hold your *gabby* relatives to the task at hand.

It is a good idea to record your meeting. Use a small cassette recorder or a video camera. As chairperson, neither you nor your recording secretary will remember or understand all of the topics discussed and suggestions made.

If your home town is more convenient for a majority of family members, select it for your gathering. Suggestions may surface to change the location of the reunion. Make certain that the new location is convenient to you as chairperson. It is best to have family members or friends located in the selected city, they can provide *inside scoop* to bargains and places to avoid.

Call the Chamber of Commerce and Visitors Bureau of the city you select and request enough copies of information on activities for each committee member. It is a good idea to tell the person you speak with that you are planning your reunion and are seriously considering their city. Cities now view reunions as ways to increase revenue. Your inquiry will be well received, especially in your home town.

AREA COORDINATORS

If your family members are not centrally located, instead of appointing committee members, why not solicit area coordinators. Get a small U. S. map and place it in a notebook labeled "Family Reunion 1995 (Appendix I). Place a mark on each state where a large percentage of family members reside. Get someone to volunteer in each location. When you have information to share, announce it by way of each area coordinator.

Some family members will be difficult to contact. Area coordinators can be responsible for making contact with these relatives. Numerous attempts by mail to each unresponsive family member can deplete your postage allotment.

It is nice to have access to this group of relatives as area coordinators. They can provide advice and brainstorm with you when you have exhausted solutions to problems.

CENTRAL LOCATION

YOUR HOME? I think not! If you have a huge home with acres of land, then consider it. But why drive yourself nuts? If you want to schedule one of the activities at your home, plan an outdoor or even an indoor affair; however, GET PLENTY OF HELP!

When you schedule _down time_ or _free time_ use it to rest. You and your committee need to replenish your energy. Another point of emphasis, if you own a motel, then allow relatives to stay with you for the reunion. Otherwise, limit traffic in your home. You will have enough activity.

The actual reunion location, in addition to being safe, should be convenient with reasonable rates and a swimming pool. Once you book a set number of rooms, most hotels will provide a meeting room at no additional cost. However, do not place yourself in a corner regarding the number of rooms anticipated.

Regardless of the site you select, remember that someone will have a favorite hotel, motel, or bed and breakfast. Some people will stay with friends or other relatives. Don't be offended by any of these practices. People do what is most convenient for them.

Even though you arrange some meals, you cannot possibly provide them all. Here is an important hint: Select a hotel near nationally known eateries; menu and prices are varied and reasonable. Plus, relatives can utilize this time away from scheduled activities to be alone, call home, shampoo their hair or just be a couch potato for awhile. Select a hotel that accommodates your needs. Demand options. Hotels have a margin of flexibility, especially when revenue is involved.

DATES

First, look at your calendar. What dates are best for you? Double check the dates, make sure you are available. You are the chair or co-chair, on the day of the reunion, please realize, if you must be absent, Murphy just may decide to wreak havoc. Your hours of hard work won't be identifiable.

Is there an important date in your family? Grandparents' anniversary, traditional family meeting dates, concert, or annual city-wide celebrations provide excellent reasons for selecting reunion dates. Combine a city-wide festival with your reunion. If it is fun for city residents; it will add fun moments to your reunion. It will seem as though the city's planners are on your side and at no added expense to you.

THEME

Discovering your family's theme is an exciting activity. You can keep the same theme each year, or you can form a committee to revise it. See Chapter 9 for guidelines.

COLORS

You need a vote on this idea from your committee and some other family members. You will not get a consensus, what you will get are strong opinions.

The colors you select, usually two, should dominate your location, tee-shirts, and most special projects. Make sure that the colors compliment each other and most of your relatives. Your celebration should represent brightness and warmth. Black and brown is a combination that conjures images of dullness and depression. Lively combinations draw attention and add flair to tee-shirts.

Remember males in your family when you select colors. A combination of pink and lavender is not fair to them. You could take wearing reunion colors a step further. During worship services, most men wear ties. Have at least one reunion color that men can wear. If lavender and pink are your colors, a majority of men in your family might have a problem.

INITIAL INFORMATION

Where do your family members reside? Who are they? These are very significant questions because you don't want to overlook anyone.

Just how far back in history do you go? That is really up to your family. Your grandparent's line is a good starting place. However, it is best to go back a generation, find out as much as you can about that generation, then keep going back until you exhaust all possibilities of ever finding additional information (Chapter 10).

How will you do this? Start with your parent (the line you are celebrating) and branch out. As you meet with area coordinators, allocate time to discuss your linkages so that you can pinpoint addresses and telephone numbers.

INTRODUCTORY LETTER

Mail an introductory letter (Appendix A) once preliminary plans are made. Some people will need LOTS OF TIME. For others, a couple of months is sufficient. Ideally, if you are planning a huge reunion (going back generations), and it is your first, give family members at least a year's notice.

Compose an introductory letter. Make it as enthusiastic as possible. It will be your sales pitch. Welcome and cheer the start of your upcoming event.

Encourage, no, beg each member to participate. Give the location, dates, anticipated events and approximate fee at least three to four months before the event. Also, list names of committee members/coordinators. Include an approximate date for your next correspondence and a deadline to pay fees. Keep it light and non-threatening!

How many mailings are enough, ten, 20? No, at least two before the event, three mailings are commendable.

1. Keep the first letter very simple. Include dates and future plans.
2. Final or mid-planning letter contains more

specific information regarding itinerary and registration fee.

3. Final letter confirms itinerary. This is your last chance to make a sales pitch for relatives to share their abilities with you for scheduling entertainment.

REGISTRATION FEES

If your reunion is longer than one day, and if it involves many activities, a registration fee is appropriate. As Chairperson, you must become a creative genius on this topic. You must set a fee. At the same time, do not scare off anyone with the fee you set.

Even though you announce a deadline for paying registration fees, encourage family members to pay as soon as possible, in part or whole. You will incur expenses long before your deadline.

Keep meticulous records of each person's payments. It is a good idea to provide copies of fees paid by each individual during registration.

Two methods for fee assessment are suggested: one, individual registrations; and two, family registrations. With family registrations, it is possible to end up in the RED if some families have several children and others have a couple. The recommended method is individual registration fees.

INDIVIDUAL REGISTRATION FEES

When individuals are accessed a fee, all expenses are

totaled and divided among the number of expected attendees or rates for individuals are added and the sum becomes the fee for adults and admissions and other charges for children are added. The sum obtained becomes the fee for children.

Any fee you set will cause some discussion. Discuss this topic carefully with committee members and area coordinators. *Set a fee and collect it, or you will pay out of your pocket when people show up.*

RATES INCLUDED HERE ARE INSERTED AS EXAMPLES. THEY DO NOT REPRESENT IDEAL REGISTRATION FEES.

Method One - Estimated Number of Participants

1. bus tour	(43 people)	$515-12.50
2. breakfast	(75)	600-8.00
3. get acqua.	(75)	600-6.67
4. banquet	(80)	1000-12.50
5. fun run	t-shirts	650-8.33
6. lunch	(75)	320-4.26
7. breakfast	(75)	400-5.33
8. miscellaneous	(80)	400-5.00

TOTAL PER ADULT REGISTRANT-$55 - 65.00

Method Two - Per activity

1. bus tour $7.00
2. breakfast   5.00
3. get acqua. 5.00
4. banquet   9.00

5. tee shirt   7.00
6. lunch   5.00
7. dinner   7.00
8. misc.   5.00

REGISTRATION FEE PER ADULT - $50.00

A child should pay less than an adult. For the same reunion example above, each child should pay:

1. bus tour   12.00
2. breakfast   2.00
3. get acquainted session   4.00
4. banquet   5.75
5. fun run   3.00
6. lunch   2.00
7. breakfast   1.00
8. miscellaneous   4.00

TOTAL PER CHILD 5 AND UNDER - $20.00; 6-12, $35.00; OVER 12, SAME AS ADULTS

WAYS TO DECREASE REGISTRATION FEES:

1. get a family member(s) or agencies in town to sponsor an activity - bus tour
2. offer one continental breakfast
3. picnic style lunch
4. decrease cost of banquet meal
5. get a family member to contribute postage

REGISTRATION PACKAGES

Whether you organize a formal or informal reunion, printed material helps with dissemination of information. Include as much information as possible on one sheet. Or provide 10 sheets per person. Remember expenses if you should.

Packages can be business size envelopes, colored paper bags purchased from a discount store or cloth bags with your reunion name or theme on them. Regardless of style, include the following information:

1. receipt
2. itinerary
3. information on optional side tours, places of worship, restaurants
4. your address and phone number
5. tide-over package (soda, candy bar or cookies, fruit, restaurant *discount coupons)*
6. tickets for prizes
7. financial report (best to distribute during business meeting)
8. stuffers

The first four items are essential; five, six and eight are nice to do. Make receipts on a computer, typewriter or purchase a receipt book from a discount store.

The itinerary should be very specific. When it is completed (but not copied for the reunion), give a copy to a child and a second copy to an adult. See if questions are asked about activities. If questions are not answered with a simple explanation, you probably need to revise your itinerary. Remember, you have worked with this baby for a long time. You know what you mean, but do others.

Information listed on lines 3 and 4 should be included on one sheet of paper. Distribute badges or name tags during registration. Remind everyone to wear their name tag to each activity. Purchase gummed name tags or have tags made (according to your budget). Gummed labels are great because they are inexpensive.

Items included on line 5 are tide-over items. If a muncher is in your group, these items will tide the person over until the next scheduled meal. Some relatives will arrive after restaurants and eateries have closed. If so, these items are a welcomed surprise. For late arrivals, place registration packages in their rooms.

Area merchants, city officials, and your committee are resources for locating no-cost and low-cost items that make great "stuffers." These items can be any memento of your reunion location a button, bumper sticker, decal, spoon, a plastic cup, sun visor. Some businesses and even banks will often donate promotional items.

PRIZES

Line six requires much discussion. In addition to awarding a prize for "most information shared" (Chapter 4), you can provide prizes for first registration fee paid, first to arrive, oldest and youngest attendee, most children, traveled farthest distance, lost most weight since last reunion, most improved health since last meeting. Create your own winning reasons.

This activity provides a wealth of fun. Place tickets in registration packages. Instruct each person to write their names on back of the ticket, if you have not done so already. Prizes can be awarded each day.

This is the fun part! I enjoy hiding prizes, under chair legs, under seats, 10th person to walk through the door, etc. Here is an example:

> You have 10 mugs to award as prizes, color a letter in your reunion theme or place your initials inside a letter on the itinerary (you know your handwriting). Announce what you have done to your family. Watch, as people scurry to find their itineraries (never to misplace them again).

Prizes do not come from prize heaven. Get them donated or allocate a few dollars in your budget to purchase nice regional or other gifts.

Establish rules; try these. When a person wins, their ticket is not returned to the *prize box*. A person cannot win more than one prize, only one per household, age can be a factor, or must be present to win. Winning a prize does not prohibit the person from receiving an award.

Here is an attention getting idea. Announce your criteria during the *Get Acquainted Session*, when you review your itinerary with your entire group. Decorate a box with brightly colored paper and make sure every person is aware of its location. After you explain the prize box, get everyone present to place their tickets in the box. Immediately, award one or two unique prizes.

Awarding prizes is optional. As you read, you are probably thinking, *now, all of that is not necessary*. Try it, just once. The results are amazing. This activity will keep your relatives on time. I have witnessed unbelievable results when even unwrapped, extraordinary key chains are given away. The element of *winning* is the motivating factor and not the actual prize.

I love this prize, and your family will enjoy it as well. Locate an artist, of the aspiring type, who draws caricatures, negotiate a fee and a contract. Pay for 5-10 caricatures, or pay for one hour. Some artists can complete a caricature in five to 10 minutes. Award these as prizes. Arrange for the artist to be available for other interested family members. You control the exchange of money, and charge a couple of dollars extra per drawing. The additional money can either defray the cost of your original booking with the artist or serve as investment capitol for your family (Chapter 11).

RECORDS

Provide a receipt for each person. It is a good idea to place them in registration packages.

Purchase a notebook and record each person's name, amount paid, how paid, when received, and their address and telephone number. Collect receipts for each and every item purchased for the reunion and for each contract signed. You will need this information during the business meeting.

When items are purchased, pay by receipts. Do not deduct expenses from registration fees. Paying by submitted receipts eliminates problems.

BUSINESS MEETING

Do not, I repeat, do not schedule this essential part of your reunion for the evening of your last day. A majority of your relatives will not attend. Their reasons are justified. Everybody is tired by that time. The fun is over. Many people must return to work or their departure flight is early.

A business meeting transforms your family's reunion into a power meeting for adults and children. Yes, children *must* attend. Too noisy you say, too bad. Appoint them to distribute the meeting's agenda, to monitor the tape recorder, to vote on issues, to give advice from a child's perspective. Children must grow into being important.

These little people understand much more than some parents and other people give them credit for. Tell your five year older that money left over will be deposited into savings accounts for the family's children. Suddenly, this child who could not understand why kicking the table is distracting, will ask pertinent questions: *Why do we need so many balloons?* Or get this one: *What is my share?*

There are numerous reasons for having a business meeting. Number one is to clarify any misgivings regarding finances. Other equally important reasons are to plan the next reunion; choose a chairperson; to revamp family plans; to elect officers, and to organize your family's history. Use a simple format for your business report:

1. number of registrations paid
2. number of registration fees with a
   remaining balance
3. cost of t-shirts
4. prizes
5. meals
   a. breakfast
   b. lunch
   c. bar-be-cue

    d. miscellaneous

    e. banquet

6. tours

    a. city-wide

    b. adjacent locations

7. copies

8. postage

9. miscellaneous

10. donations

    a. relative A

    b. relative B

Separate expenditures from money received. In the above example, total items one and ten and report as cash on hand.

CHECKING ACCOUNT

Call several banks in town and inquire about a "no fee" checking account for short-term use. If none offer this service, suggest it. Numerous banks across the country offer this kind of service to the community.

Do not keep registration fees at home. The money is too accessible; it will be gone before you know it. Deposit every penny as soon as it arrives. Get someone on your reunion committee to be a second signer on the account.

ACKNOWLEDGEMENTS

This point is germane to survival. Acknowledge each person who served on the committee and anyone else who assisted at the last minute. Here is an idea. At your banquet, or business meeting, ask all persons to stand and remain standing during acknowledgements. First, call committee members, last minute helpers and please find some way to acknowledge children and young adults for participating. When almost all persons present have been named, ask those seated to stand. Acknowledge them for supporting your family's efforts to remain a united family.

Do not commit the ultimate faux pas. Forget to acknowledge suppliers who gave you a discount and they may not provide that generosity in the future. Written thank you notes are in order. Besides, it helps to verify donations for tax time. There are still other notes to write. Acknowledge the assistance of friends and acquaintances who assist you in seemingly small ways.

Another point, decide on some unique way for relatives to identify committee members. Assign children as co-helpers (not just your children and immediate family). Purchase the same kind of identifying "symbol" for them as well. Everybody uses flowers and buttons. Try something different: bold hats (add ribbons or flowers), ribbons, jackets, aprons, armbands. This way, family members who need assistance can find people other than you.

IMPORTANT POINTS:

1. Remember that your plans should consider your average family members and not the few who can afford anything their hearts desire.

2. Communicate with your committee members.

3. If relatives live in several geographic regions, appoint area coordinators who will keep relatives in these areas informed and encourage participation.

NOTES:

_____

_____

_____

_____

_____

_____

_____

_____

_____

_____

_____

_____

_____

_____

_____

_____

NOTES:

_____

_____

_____

_____

_____

_____

_____

_____

_____

_____

_____

_____

_____

_____

_____

_____

_____

*A man hath no better thing under the sun
than to eat, and to drink, and to be merry.*
-Bible, *Ecclesiastes, 8:15*

C
H
A
P
T
E
R

THREE:

*Let Us Break Bread Together:
Count The Many Ways*

When people get together, regardless of the occasion, nothing melts the ice better than food and drink. Numerous methods exist for consuming meals: picnics, bar-be-cues, fish fries, banquets, brunch, lunch, breakfast, dinner, tea, cocktails, reception, plus others. Schedule the affair at someone's home, a backyard, park, restaurant, church, or club. You get the picture, so be creative. People just want food that looks and tastes good prepared by reputable people.

Family gatherings are not characteristic of American families alone. Regardless of a family's ethnic or cultural heritage, getting together with relatives to renew relationships is a common practice everywhere in the world. In other cultures, these gatherings occur more often, and for even others, families never leave their birth location.

Encourage ethnic foods during these meetings. When families meet, cultural specialties should be included. This is an inexpensive and enjoyable way to recapture your heritage.

You can make your reunion spectacular by being creative with meals and by incorporating other activities at mealtime. *How? By entertaining each other.* After the invocation, what happens next? Eat and leave? I think not. *It is show time!* (Chapter 4).

Turn an ordinary meal into a spectacular affair that compares to a state dinner or an organization's annual banquet. Explore and exploit family talent. Encourage your family's children to participate. In fact, put them out front. You will be surprised by what they do, and by the long-term effects of focusing on them.

COORDINATION

Dear chairperson, your duties are not over. For each scheduled activity, assign a coordinator. As chairperson, you must keep everything flowing and on time. For more formal affairs, dinners and banquets, an emcee is essential.

Look inside your family for a dynamic personality. Pair a female and a male emcee, or a child and an adult. This part of your program holds promise of being a number one memorable event.

Request a microphone and a podium. Have a *head table* and invite the mayor or his designee, you of course, chairperson, honoree, emcee(s), and committee members (optional).

VIDEO TAPES AND PHOTOS

Remember to record significant portions of all events. However, at the same time, do remember to be courteous when videotaping. No one wants their photo taken when they have just gorged their mouths with a piece of food. It is not necessary to capture every moment. Besides, who has time to view 24 hours of tape? Candid shots are always best.

Inform your photographer of preferences for photos and video taping. Don't over scrutinize this part, if you do, some special moments will be lost. Edit video tapes if continuous recording is what you desire.

PICNICS

Don't forget to post signs if you are in a crowded park. Add balloons to get attention. Decorate tables and trees in reunion colors. Serve food that will not spoil (old favorite-chicken or ethnic specialties).

Remind every family to bring a blanket and outdoor games. Volleyball, horse shoes, card games and croquet offer a variety for the energetic and the *conservative energy spender.*

If reserved areas are not allowed, designate someone to

arrive early to stake out a place for your picnic. Do not assume that plenty of space will be available.

BAR-BE-CUE

Whether its in a park or someone's backyard, everybody *enjoys a bar-be-cue*. There is one catch. You will need food for more people in a short period of time. Designate official bar-be-cuers. Whoever is assigned this task should actually start cooking hours before the activity begins.

Inform neighbors of your activities to temper problems. A group of people outdoors enjoying themselves will talk and laugh; sound carries. Add music, add parking infractions, what you have are potential problems. Try to anticipate possible problems. Invite your neighbors as a gesture of friendliness.

Again, decorate the area with your reunion colors. Use umbrellas, candles, spot lights, Christmas lights, party lights, and torches. Include music, watch the volume though. Do not aggravate your neighbors. Always place a sign-in book in a prominent location.

FISH FRY

Get ready for the GREASE. Prepare a fish that most people like; somehow get your hands on a fish cooker or deep fryers. Because of the odor, schedule this activity outside.

Arrange tables with umbrellas, park benches, and chairs in configurations for people to gather and talk. Place condiments on each table or in a central location. Wrap small boxes in reunion colors and place identical condiments in each. This strategy helps prevent accidents. Trash receptacles are an absolute necessity around your yard or park. Include handiwipes on your list of items needed.

Do not forget your reunion colors. Use varying sizes of straw trays to hold bread, desserts, and other items. Line trays with paper or fabric in reunion colors; place plastic wrap on top - add food item.

Serve the usual fried fish and other family meat favorites, and accompaniments: cole slaw, baked beans, potato or garden salad, hush puppies, dill pickles, vidalia onions, sodas, melons and desserts.

BANQUET

For a more eloquent dining occasion, plan a banquet in conjunction with a talent or fashion show or better yet, a dance. Have someone speak (10-15 minutes) on your family's history or other topic. Arrange to have this meal catered. Schedule it for the meeting room at your hosting hotel. Ask to use the banquet room free with a set number of reserved rooms. If the banquet room is inadequate or nonexistent, look elsewhere in your community for a location with ambience.

Encourage family members to dress in their best finery. You'll be surprised at the difference this change in format makes, going from casual to dressy. This meal is usually scheduled toward the end of your family's time together.

Add music to the affair. Expensive you think. Contact the music department at your local college or university, inquire about musicians to your liking, chamber music, jazz, contemporary, rock. The fee is usually very meager. If your budget will allow it, hire a local band or try this, get a DJ for music after dinner.

BRUNCH

This is an ideal meal, if you and your family have been on the go. This meal will allow time for "sleeping in" while providing flexibility for you in food selections. It omits preparing breakfast by combining the meal with lunch, but at a later hour than breakfast and earlier than lunch.

Quiches, meats with sauce, fruit, and rolls of all kinds highlight the menu. Once again, table decorations are limitless.

BREAKFAST

There is no way you can please everyone for any meal. If there is one to have in a restaurant, this one is it. Fast food chains usually have reasonable breakfast bars. Ask for mid-week rates for a large group. Maybe management will comply. Decide what is best for your family.

Breakfast at home is *always* special. It provides a gentle *letdown* at the end of your activities. Plus, it allows a relaxed opportunity, if scheduled on the last morning, for everyone to bid farewell.

LUNCH

Keep lunch simple. Serve two meats. Better yet, make a deal with a restaurant and add the cost in the registration fee.

If you schedule a bus tour for your family, get friends to prepare a meal for the trip. Purchase one of the following items for each person: napkins, a paper bag (in one of your reunion colors if possible), a soda, chips, sandwich or chicken, fruit, a fork if serving a salad, and pastry. The results is a nice bag lunch to tide the group over until dinner.

DINNER

Whatever you serve for Sunday dinner should be okay for a reunion dinner. Just remember to keep items served simple yet prepared in a special way. Again, consider a caterer for this meal.

If a dinner is planned inside your home, do not serve food with sauces or drinks that will stain your carpet. Avoid cherry or any dark berry dessert. Serve sodas, punch and wine that are clear or light in color. Accidents will happen.

If this meal is held in your home, use large ribbons and streamers to decorate. Place a banner somewhere in your yard and a smaller one inside your home. A sign-in roster in a prominent location is essential for keeping track of visitors. In town relatives may not attend regular meals (breakfast or lunch). However, a late evening meal with activities will get their attention.

TEA

Not many people schedule a tea during a reunion, but remember your family traditions when you plan activities. Planning a tea for a large number should be simple. Remember to serve a variety of desserts, teas, punches and coffee. Arrange chairs to facilitate communication. Again, plan for increased attendance. Place a sign-in roster in a prominent location.

RECEPTION

The ideal time to have a semi-reception is on the *sign-in day or registration period*. This is the evening most people arrive for the festivities. Something to drink and light foods to consume are okay.

During the reception is an appropriate time to schedule a *Get Acquainted Session* (Chapter 4). Relatives get to know each other the very first night instead of waiting a day or two to discover relationships.

COCKTAILS

Why not! But do not forget that children will attend. What will you serve them? This activity adds an expense. Plan for each person to consume at least two of whatever they drink, and at least four different finger foods.

Since dinner is on the way, keep hors d'oeuvres simple. When you make plans, remember your family's philosophy and habits. You do not want to cause bitter feelings among teetotalers.

SUMMARY

Get your committee to assist you with meal plans. It really does not matter what you serve. Just remember to encourage conversation, light up your backyard or park, provide sufficient chairs, and decorate all locations with your reunion colors.

IMPORTANT POINTS:

1. *Place a sign in roster or book at each activity. This lets you know who stopped by to say hello to the family. In town relatives usually attend meals with activities planned during late evening.*
2. *Remember, that some relatives are on special diets. You cannot possibly cater to them all. If you serve a fried meat serve one that is baked and always have diet sodas and unsweetened tea on hand.*
3. *Make huge banners and print them in reunion colors or make a black and white banner and color in letters with reunion colors.*
4. *Schedule your dinner or banquet in an unusual place. What about the local opera house, theater, or museum? Museums welcome opportunities to get visitors. Most require that you hire security guards for the evening. If the cost is not a problem for you. Do it! The ambience is unbelievably nice!*

NOTES:

_____

_____

_____

_____

_____

_____

_____

_____

_____

_____

_____

_____

_____

*If a man does not make new acquaintances
as he advances through life, he will soon find
himself left alone.* Samuel Johnson, quoted in
Boswell's, Life of Johnson, 1755

C
H
A
P
T
E
R

FOUR:

Planning a Get Acquainted Session

Not many people in this world are totally familiar with all of their relatives. It is almost impossible to keep track of family additions when most relatives do not live close by. New names seem to appear at every gathering. Somewhere, cousins and other relatives exist that you know absolutely nothing about.

Have you ever met someone who, for some gut reason, has strong family features and just puts a question in your mind that *you are related?* Or have you discovered a relative through casual conversation with a once-thought stranger? Or what about this situation. Suppose you actually date someone and later discover you are relatives. What an awkward situation. Get to a reunion fast and discover your relatives.

Now that relatives have driven, flown, taken a train, ship or had someone drive them to the reunion, what is next? Light conversation only lasts so long. This little speech comes at an appropriate time to convince you to take advantage of every opportunity to get to know your relatives and encourage conversation.

It is wonderful to laugh and enjoy good food. Again, small talk about tasty morsels can last just so long. By the time you have consumed more than your share, and you really feel comfortable with your new found relatives, it is time to go home. This time, plan activities that enhance discovery of your wealth of relationships. Wealth is not always measured in money. Support, love and kinship are actually more valuable and more lasting.

Sometimes hindrances in family communication date back before the present relatives were born. So questions abound. Why can't we visit Aunt Mary? Are there other cousins I haven't been told about? Who was that on the phone? She insisted that she is my aunt? And on and on it goes.

ADD STRUCTURE

Spontaneous conversation is fantastic for those who are gifted conversationalist and who are secure in their setting. But what about the family member who visits and is a stranger to everyone? It is best to plan activities that decrease initial stress for all concerned.

I met a cousin and her family for the first time at a reunion. She had not communicated with anyone on a regular basis that I am aware of. She introduced herself and her family to the entire group and continued on as though she had been a part of everyone's daily life. Every family has members who are exactly like my cousin; no matter where they are communication comes easy.

Few people have that kind of personality. So don't rely on spontaneous conversation as a method of getting relatives acquainted. Planned activities work well for the reserved person or the relative who is related to someone once shunned by part of the family. It is time to end the feud at your reunion. Allow the dissolution to occur naturally, and it will. Work toward getting people together.

Exceptions exist to this altruistic approach. If a devastating situation occurred in your family, and you decide that someone should mediate a session, look outside your family for that person. An unbiased party is essential.

Simple hurt relations can mend themselves when relatives get together and realize that some situations are nonsense. But devastating occurrences require a non-involved person to lead discussions to get rid of anger. Again, *if* it is possible. Some rifts are very complex. Get on with your reunion, you might forego the attendance of relatives who are part of the family's inner circle as well.

ON TO GETTING ACQUAINTED

Assign partners for this activity. Make it easy, put names in a hat. Each person gets a partner when the first name is called. For instance, Pam Sam pulls John Sam's name.

Pam's name is still in the hat, when it is pulled, because she has a partner already, discard her name.

Pam simply knows that John is her cousin; the two have never met. It is their responsibility to discover their relationship, find out about work and recreational histories. Later, maybe 10-15 minutes, each person must introduce the opposite person. Set a time limit. Three minutes each is enough. Yes, assign a time keeper. If your family is huge, divide this very important session into parts I and II with a break in between. It is very important to plan this session for the very beginning of your reunion.

To plan this kind of activity at the end of your time together is anticlimactic. It is too late then to take advantage of precious time to allow newly found relationships to develop.

At the end of this chapter, write down a few ideas that you can implement to guide, not lead, conversation. Additionally, list ideas for a structured way to introduce relatives to each other. Try the ones listed below.

ACTIVITIES

Number One

In your newsletter (if you decide to write one) or information letter, challenge family members to bring memorabilia with them and to obtain information about their family of origin. Offer prizes to the household that brings the most information. Also offer prizes to family members who talk to the most family members about their history and how it connects with theirs. Of course, you should provide a check list of possible relationship combinations and offer prizes to persons who discover the most during the evening.

Number Two

Hypothetically, lets suppose your paternal great grand parents had four children. Your father's mother (one of the four children), married and had three children: your father and his two sisters. You have one brother and a sister, and each of your two aunts had four children. It is then up to family members to discover their relationship with your great grandparents. Four lines of relationships exist because your great grandparents had four children.

It is reasonable to assume that you will be familiar with your fathers linkage, but what about your great grandparents other three children? Becoming acquainted with the unfamiliar family line offers a challenge. Plus, relatives realize when they are not among the group of popular or familiar relations. Bring everyone *in* if it is possible.

Number Three

Another interesting activity that brings older and wizened members of your family into the spotlight is for them to introduce their immediate family members. Your father's parents would be responsible for introducing their children, grandchildren, and great grandchildren. The same is true for your grandparent's siblings.

What is appropriate to share? Whatever comes to mind. Remember, your goal is to learn about your relatives, especially if you are not around them continuously. Names, birth order, hobbies, occupations, city of residence, and something that is special about each person yields excellent information.

Number Four

Yet another activity entails assignment of households or families of origin to tables. Have them bring old family photos and memorabilia and share the story that surrounds the object or picture. You must be organized because this activity could take two days. Give each family a time limit. No more than three to 10 minutes is reasonable (time constraints depend on scheduled activities and size of your family).

While history is being shared, assign someone or get a volunteer to serve as the family's historian. Start a family album. Plan to pass the album on to the chairperson of your next reunion. Ask for duplicates of rare photos to start a family album or video.

IMPORTANT POINTS:

1. *Hire someone to place old photos on videotape.*
2. *Save time and money and hire the same person, if possible, to videotape your Get Acquainted Session.*
3. *Assign someone to take notes.*
4. *Set up tables for family groups to share information.*
5. *Make out a list of possible relations, or add nicknames of grandparents, wedding dates, favorite sayings and have a semi-scavenger hunt.*

NOTES:

NOTES:

_____

_____

_____

_____

_____

_____

_____

_____

_____

_____

_____

_____

_____

_____

_____

_____

_____

_____

C
H
A
P
T
E
R

FIVE:

Tours and Other Outdoor Activities

Now that you have your family members together, get out and travel around. See the sights. Even though local relatives have visited scheduled locations numerous times, encourage them to participate as well. Out of town relatives provide a fresh perspective, and you will strengthen new friendships as you travel together.

A good place to start is where your great grandparents or grandparents grew up. Try to visualize the town as it was years ago. Ask a local librarian to assist you to find old photos of the town around the time your relatives lived in the area.

Preassign someone to contact the library or visit and find out about the town during the years your relatives first settled there. If your investigation will not allow retrieval of history, provide as much information as you can about the town. These two activities will help you get a *feel* for the kind of life your relatives lived.

FREE TIME

Do not attempt to account for every minute during the reunion. In fact, schedule *free time* during the middle of your time together. Provide information on optional tours. Your relatives will come to the area with plans of their own to visit friends and opposite line relatives. And some relatives just want to relax. Take advantage of this opportunity to get much needed rest or to check on remaining activities.

SCHEDULED TOURS

With your committee/area coordinators, make note of historic locations and other points of interest. You cannot possibly visit all area attractions; select as many as your fee will allow, and the hours and feet can endure.

If a food processing company exists in your area, include it on your tour. These companies give samples to take with you and to taste in their company. For instance, Tom's Foods gives samples of candy and cookies to groups, and it is interesting to see how snacks are mass produced.

Schedule a tour of the town and adjacent area by boat if possible. Many boat city tours have meals and dancing as part of their attraction.

PARKS

Is there a fun park in your area? If admission tickets are reasonable, and if it is unusual, include it in your package. Do remember, if your town is small and your relatives all reside in large cities, visiting the family home site may be more interesting than touring a tiny fun park that numbers in the thousands where they reside.

SPECIAL TOUR

The next point may seem gruesome to some, but you will be as amazed as I was when I experienced a cousin's connection with our grandmother. After a funeral for an Aunt, a cousin asked to see our Grandmother's grave. As we gathered, my cousin kneeled and cried as though our Grandmother had just died. It was almost as though the reality of Grandmother's life and death *connected* for her. When it was over she said, "I don't remember Grandmother, but now I feel as though I've at least touched her life by being near her grave."

Maybe your relatives will not respond in this way. If requested, provide opportunities for out-of-town relatives to visit family burial grounds.

OPTIONAL SIDE TOURS

Insert brochures on optional tours in registration packages. There is no way to schedule tours to all area activities. Provide free time and information on area attractions, your relatives can venture out on their own.

If it is not possible to obtain brochures for each person, place a second table adjacent to the registration table and label it *OTHER ATTRACTIONS* or similar name. Staple or tape the front side and back of a brochure on an easel or table. Do the same for a city map.

TIPS

Try to visit facilities and attractions that are interesting but do not require half your budget for admission. No matter how inviting a reunion may seem, a steep registration fee will keep you and others from discovering vital relationships. In today's economy, money is a factor.

If prices are beginning to get unreasonable in planning this affair, call local churches and synagogues and ask if their buses are for rent. If so, schedule the most reasonable and most reliable for your tour transportation.

IMPORTANT POINTS:

1. *If your time together is limited, limit tours, remember this is your time to discover relationships. Although tours and other activities, break the ice, they can inhibit meaningful conversation.*
2. *Winter time is not a good season for older people if outdoor activities dominate your agenda. Determine time required for each tour (don't want to tire people out), location of toilets, age of people participating. Then again, do not underestimate the will of older people. A reunion may just be the medicine to keep them going long after younger relatives have quit. I have seen it happen.*

NOTES:

_____

_____

_____

_____

_____

_____

_____

_____

_____

_____

_____

_____

_____

_____

_____

C
H
A
P
T
E
R

SIX:

Special Activities

Some special activities do not carry a price tag. The surprise factor that accompany them include immeasurable benefits. I have listed several activities in this chapter. Brainstorm with your committee to think of others. If you think these ideas are a bit flamboyant, think again. Your family members will realize how special they are to you when you go to the trouble to place emphasis on your reunion and relationship with them.

Now is an excellent occasion to pay homage to a

deserving relative. Honor someone for unspoken deeds. Have each relative complete a copy of the *Family Inventory* (Appendix F). Note unusual activities and provide kudos for that unsung family hero.

PROCLAMATION

Get the mayor of your city to proclaim a day in your family's honor. It is a simple procedure, but it will require that you do a bit of writing.

You can get a proclamation format from your mayor's office. This is usually true for all cities and small towns. Complete necessary information. The mayor's secretary will do the rest.

If a proclamation format does not exist for families, request a copy designated for an organization. Use either form as a guide. Below is an example of statements contained in a proclamation:

Whereas the Mayor of _____ acknowledges the _____ family for its years of support in this community. May it be known to all that this _____ day of _____ 19__ is known as the _____ Family Day in honor of _____

Additional statements that begin with whereas follow the first and before the last statement. Invite the mayor or his representative to attend your dinner. Have the proclamation presented to you as chairperson or to the oldest living member of your family, or to the relative who has proven to be most supportive of family efforts.

KEY TO THE CITY

Do you have a *special family member* you want to honor for mentioned or unmentioned acts? That person can be someone who is involved in community service or who has a prestigious job who lives out of town. Again, a key could be awarded to the oldest living member of your family (who lives out of town). If the oldest person lives in town have that person accept the key on behalf of the entire family.

The same procedure used to request a proclamation is used for a key to the city. Do so well in advance of the reunion, it takes time to have these two special activities processed.

FUN RUN/WALK

What about organizing a fun run? Not just your ordinary fun run that involves only your family, but one that involves the entire city and regions beyond. If I have lost you, schedule a run or walk for your family only. Do read on. Consider this idea for your next reunion.

Does your family have a favorite charity? Maybe a family illness or disease exists. If so, research is expensive, and charitable and other non-profit organizations are always in need of additional financial assistance. Contact local organizations, explain your plans to organize a fun run with 50% of the proceeds donated to their organization. Decide on a percentage with your committee. You will probably get assistance from the organization. Money is a crucial factor these days.

Since a huge donation will go towards charity, you can publicize the event on the radio and television *free*. The selected organization and radio and television stations can assist with announcements. Get several family members to volunteer for this event. Maybe someone is a runner. Everyone walks or can ride in wheel chairs. Put everyone to work.

Contact your local runner's association. Ask them to assist with the affair. Do not allow the very thought of this activity to overwhelm you. Arrangements can be simple and time consuming. Steps to achieve your local fun run are listed below:

1. query the family for organizers
2. contact charitable organization (could also be a homeless shelter or home for battered women or abused children)
3. contact runners' organization
4. obtain city permit and get police escorts
5. contact local or nearby soft drink distributors and request support for the day
6. contact well known fast food chains and get coupons for each race finisher
7. go back to step 4, the deadline needs to be set for registrations so you will have a sure number of participants when ordering tee shirts
8. advertise the race through radio and television, the local charitable organization will have examples of public service announcements (PSAs) for you to follow
9. when you order your reunion tee-shirts, order enough for non-relatives who register for the fun run or walk.

In designing the tee-shirt, put all personal information about your family's reunion on the back. On the front, print a slogan about the charitable organization(s) you sponsor, the date, and city. Include this information on all tee-shirts.

Save extra money by making tee shirts the same color. The 50% that you keep for your family can be used in several ways: one, to defray cost of registration; two, to serve as start-up funds for a family investment (see Chapter 11); and three, to defray costs of a reunion in a *special location* (appendix E).

All tee-shirts can have the same front but a different back. Non-family participants can have part of the back design. Only family members will have tee-shirts with information that relate specifically to your reunion.

EXERCISE PROGRAM

Are you an exercise buff? Others in your family are probably engaged in some kind of program. Keep the weight off and that feeling of charged energy going even though you are on a semi-vacation.

Make arrangements for a group of you to get together. People will bring steppers, body slides, curlers, weights (free, hand and ankle), video taped programs, and all sorts of portable equipment. Plan 15, 30 and 45 minute segments for people who do not bring their usual video taped programs with them. If this does not work, the willing will take a brisk walk.

This is an ideal, general purpose topic to include on your reunion agenda. Rapid turnover of information in the health/exercise field prevent the "I've heard it before syndrome."

RAFFLE

Once again, assign several people to work with this project. Get companies to donate items for a raffle. Share with willing sponsors that part of the money generated will be awarded to a charity in their name.

Print official raffle tickets, request that each family member sell a set number. Family members are not eligible to win any of the prizes. Announce the winners during your reunion. Remaining monies can be used for start-up money for a family investment or to defray costs of the reunion itself.

FAMILY PICTURES

Hire someone to take a picture of your entire reunion group! Relatives will want copies of the photo. Get a special offer from a photographer or look to someone in the family who is in business to arrange this activity for you. Make the photos available to family members. No, not free, but at a reduced price.

Increase the price by a dollar or two. Again, discuss this strategy with committee members.

CARICATURES

You laugh. But this activity is fun and inexpensive.

People enjoy the similarity between themselves and a cartoon. All children will enjoy it, older adult children, too.

Every person present will want a caricature drawn. Let them pay for it. Provide a few as prizes. Charge a dollar or two or more than the artist charges you. Contract with the artist. You or a designee should collect the money. Deposit money left over into your family's bank for its Kids Bank or family graduation fund (Chapter 11).

MEDIA ATTENTION

Before you bolt away. *Try this*; it works. And, guess what, it is free. Call your local television station, and ask for the person in charge of public service announcements (psa's). Mail an announcement to the identified person about your reunion:

> Channel __ TV, welcomes the _____ family to its viewing area. The _____ family is celebrating its _____ Family Reunion, (dates). Family members are visiting from _____ , _____ , _____ and _____ . (Optional: Visitors are relatives of _____.)

Do the same for radio stations and your local newspaper. The outcome is worth the effort to call your local newspaper to get your *special family member* featured.

Is an older relative celebrating a birthday around the time of your reunion? Emphasize this occasion. Make a second announcement about the celebration at that time.

If the idea of publicity frightens you, think of it as a way of inviting your city of friends into your home to say hello to out-of-town relatives.

FAMILY TALENT

Every family has talented members. Assess yours for musicians, singers and dancers. Form a family rock band, jazz band, contemporary string ensemble. *You don't have to hire entertainment; your entertainment is right in your family.* Arrange a program with dinner or a banquet. Provide time for family members to display their talent.

The band idea is not possible? Arrange a choir, or even spotlight a single family member. What about a solo? No singers either. Wait, there is hope. Family members *can* read. Form a choral reading group. This kind of ensemble was very popular in the 70's; some are found on college campuses today. Have your group select a poem with a story, go from there.

CONTESTS

Get friends to serve as judges. If you plan a talent show, award prizes for the most talented, the most ridiculous act, or to the person who really tried. Always provide a category for children.

REUNION KING-AND-QUEEN

This is a nice title to bestow on the very young or older

relatives. Make up rules (fair) that fit your family. Announce your plans before the reunion. Award the title to the couple or person that exhibits positive reunion spirit. Provide a small trophy or plague. Get with your committee/area coordinators and expand this idea.

A panel, composed of friends invited to participate in your reunion activities and several committee members can serve as judges.

WORSHIP SERVICE

Although this section is last, it indeed is most important. Include information in registration packages for places to worship. It will be difficult and unreasonable to expect every relative to attend your place of worship. Extend an invitation though.

During this reunion, information included on completed Family Inventory sheets will assist the elected or volunteered chairperson to prepare for the next reunion. Information on religiosity should be assessed. Do not assume that everyone has continued to practice a former family method of worship.

SUMMARY

To some people, the activities I have described here are a bit bizarre. But why not? When families get together, extraordinary activities should be considered commonplace, especially when they are fun and restore links and assist you to discover relationships.

IMPORTANT POINTS:

1. *GET EXCITED ABOUT YOUR ASSIGNMENT! Others around you will, too! Make this meeting worth each person's time, effort and money.*
2. *As your group enters your reunion city, and especially as you leave on tours and enter along a main thoroughfare, place a huge banner at the base of an overpass, or attach it in the manner that city officials attach announcements of events. Your family will love it.*

NOTES:

_____

_____

_____

_____

_____

_____

_____

_____

_____

_____

*There is always one moment in childhood
when the door opens and lets the future in.*
-**Graham Greene**, *The Power and The Glory*

C
H
A
P
T
E
R

SEVEN:

Especially For Kids

I cannot emphasize adequately the importance of making your family's youth feel essential. In writing this manuscript, I realized how important I felt growing up. When I made suggestions, believe me, it was often, I knew I was heard. Most of them were ridiculous as I reflect on my early youth. Yet, I was heard.

I remember trying to convince my father to allow me to set a fee for my brothers to use the bathroom. I could not understand their bathroom habits: condition of the toilet seat and towels on the floor. I decided that anyone who leaves any room, especially the bathroom, in that condition should pay to use it. Let me add, I protested most when it was my turn to clean it. I went so far as to design posters. I was in the second or third grade. I was allowed to develop and grow. Did I get my father to agree to a fee? No, I could not set a fee, but I tried.

What is my point? Focus on your family of tomorrow. Give them the love and attention needed to develop into healthy adults. Provide time in your reunion for your youth. Talent is waiting for discovery.

There is a down side. Even with good intentions, when you tell your teenagers or middle school aged children about the reunion, most of them will wonder why they must meet *new* relatives. They have enough right now. Begin now, if you have not already, and get your children involved with their family history. The best way to keep a family's history and traditions revived is to involve children and young adults in organizing reunions. Another way is by planning INTERESTING activities for them.

Assure them that they will not be the only teenager present. Most important, dispel myths. Cousins in the south do not carry cotton bags on their backs or chew tobacco, and cousins in the north are not members of gangs or on drugs. Myths do exist.

New historians are essential to family longevity. When children realize that they are essential to their family line, they are more apt to participate and make astounding suggestions.

ACTIVITIES

Plan a talent show and combine it with a major meal,

plan the entertainment. Involve family members of all ages, the very young and the old young members.

Every teenager alive knows about fashions and dancing. Contact a local department store and borrow fashions. Better yet, have family members model special outfits. Get teenagers to serve as organizers and spokespersons.

For the younger set (toddlers up), involve them in any activity for the rest of the crowd. They can appreciate the following activities. All of them are loads of fun:

Egg Relay

You will need raw eggs and a spoon for each child. The child uses only one hand and must walk (brisk pace) to a designated spot and hand the egg in the spoon to their partner. One hand remains behind their back. When an egg is dropped, the child is out.

Water Balloon (or egg toss)

For this simple and exciting game, you will need balloons and water. Two rows of participants (older children and adults) must face each other several feet apart. A balloon filled with water is tossed back and forward until it gets to the end of the line. A child is considered out when the balloon breaks or drops during their turn. The winner is the last person standing without a broken (burst) balloon.

Odds and Ends Games

Just give a child a frisbee and see what they do with it. Organize a variety of races. Tie partners legs together. Again, here is an opportunity to demonstrate your creative genius. Re-create games played and popular dances (Charleston, waltz, fruge, square dancing, the bop) during your ancestors' life time.

Karoki

Is the latest craze (one of them anyway). Kids listen to music or make their own on a special cassette player or "boom box." Provide time for them to pantomime songs.

SPOTLIGHT ON YOUTH

Have someone, a teenager, arrange television style interviews. Save segments for a *REUNION VIDEO* that you sell to sponsor your next reunion. Questions can surround school, favorite dancer, singer, group, television program, college plans, hobbies, church activities, meeting relatives, and controversial topics. The teenager you assign can manage without much assistance.

Include activities that children of all ages enjoy. If you know absolutely nothing about this area, find *teen consultants* who are willing to enlighten you. When you get the youth in your family excited about its family, your line will continue to discover its links and relationships.

Do not assume that teenagers do not have knowledge or

ability to complete a task. Always provide guidance, give encouragement, and watch the task materialize.

IMPORTANT POINTS:

1. *Incorporate children, teenagers, and young adults in your plans. They have creative ideas about every situation in life. Involve them now or regret it in the future.*

NOTES:

_____

_____

_____

_____

_____

_____

_____

_____

_____

_____

_____

_____

_____

_____

_____

_____

PART II
Gathering Information

First, say to yourself what you WOULD be;
and then do what you have to.
-Epictetus, *Discourses*

C
H
A
P
T
E
R

EIGHT:

Organizing Your Investigation

This section provides introductory information for taking your reunion a step further - adding family history. Check your library for titles dedicated to family history and gathering information.

These activities will tire even the most energetic and exhilarate you at the same time as you investigate once unknown aspects of your family's life. Do not try to complete this project alone, enlist the aid of other family members.   Relatives will surprise you, so do not underestimate their willingness to help the reunion succeed. Get assistance, and GET STARTED! The sooner you begin your search the better.

ORGANIZATION

The purpose of this section is to emphasize the need for organization. If you do not focus on organization, your search will be hindered.

Where do you begin? Start with facts that are accessible; your family of origin. Write down every possible fact about your family. Question your parents and siblings. Record these facts. Use the information collected as a guide when you gather information from the rest of your family.

Refine headings and categories and set up a filing system. Purchase spiral binders with pockets, one for each household. Decide how you are going to list the material gathered. Review all headings and use codes that will not get *cold* on you. As you discover new material, add additional headings until you have exhausted all information collected.

As you begin to collect information from your immediate family members, get volunteers to do the same. Make sure that the same headings and codes are utilized. Ensure that your record keeping system is kept constant, compiling a family story, history or book becomes a matter of summarization, instead of frantically decoding information that no longer has meaning.

EQUIPMENT

Purchase these items:

1. spiral notebooks
2. pencils and pens
3. tape recorder
4. quality cassette tapes
5. batteries
6. video camera and tapes (optional)
7. manila folders (optional)

As you can see, the equipment necessary for this project is minimal unless, of course, you want to add video taping as a method of recording family history as well as collecting information. Video recorders are reasonably priced now for most people. If you do not own one, instead of making a purchase for this project, ask a relative with a video camera to serve on the committee.

OVERLOOKED SOURCES

There are many obvious sources of information that people often overlook when attempting to pull together a family history. The long forgotten, unattractive lamp stashed away in a corner in someone's house is a perfect example. Find out its source. Maybe there is a bit of history tied to the repulsive piece of iron. Read on, the following example will show you what I mean.

Betty and Ben were married forty years ago. Betty's eccentric Aunt Kate gave the couple a pewter colored lamp with a pink tasseled shade as a gift. The lamp was housed in the couple's attic until a granddaughter decided to investigate old clothes for her wardrobe. She found out that the lamp, odd thing, was approximately one hundred years old. By the way, the pewter turned out to be silver. Even better than that, inside the lamp, wrapped in delicate handkerchiefs, was a locket on a gold chain. The locket had a diamond and ruby on its face.

This rare discovery could have ended in tragedy. The lamp could have been sent to an auction or dumped in the garbage. Look around your home and the homes of your elderly relatives. You may not find a treasure of monetary value stashed away. But the information you discover will provide insight to the past - your relatives' personalities, their likes and dislikes; hobbies and items collected.

Numerous sources exist for retrieving information. A few are included here. Your best source of information, it would seem, is an older relative. most of the time this is true, but not always. Corroborate a relative's story, especially if a clue is given that their recollection may be confused. Ask relatives for Bibles, old letters, pictures, birth and death certificates, military papers, any source of information that would link you with your past.

In talking to an older relative, any relative or family friend, record the information exactly as it is told to you. *Do not interpret the information; and do not paraphrase it.* Since you probably were not alive during the period of history being shared, make sure you take notes, ask questions if the information does not *click*. Be careful, do not insult a person's integrity who is straining to remember facts. Make a second visit if necessary.

BIBLES

Don't overlook the family Bible. If pages are torn, place the Bible on a flat surface in a well lighted area and see if you can approximate pages. Depending on the Bible's age, records may require time to read because of fading. Do your best to get through the damage. Most people were sticklers about recording information in the family Bible. Check for other Bibles. Did your family donate one to a church following a death? If so, it may still be in the church archives.

CHURCH RECORDS

Most churches kept records of some kind. Vast information awaits your retrieval. Try to obtain permission to examine files. Look through sick lists, records of dues, tithes, trustees, members of organizations, baptisms, birth and wedding announcements. Why? This information provides clues to life activities. Unlike today, the church was a major source of entertainment, support and worship.

Find the oldest living member of a church if records do not exist, or are in total disarray. Ask that person if they remember your relatives. Older persons often require time to recount the past. It may be necessary to make a second visit.

GRAVE SIGHTS

Years ago, families selected special locations as burial

sights. Find out if your family owned plots in the church cemetery. Entire families can be found buried in the same location. Research church affiliations and city and state records of old burial sights.

Recordings of both birth and death years are found on headstones. Depending on the status of headstones when erected, exposure to harshness of weather and other environmental factors, you may not be able to read the information. If this is the case, a headstone RUBBING or MARKING will make it easier to read the erosion.

Place a large sheet piece of paper on the headstone, preferably white, 8 X 14.5, and rub crayon or lead pencil over the eroded area. When done with a spot, simply move the paper and start again. Remember to keep the paper going in the direction of the part that is readable.

OLD PAPERS

Have you ever visited a relative, or even a friend and it seems quite possible that every piece of paper the person received, purchased or touched is still in their possession? Whalla! What a treasure you have stumbled across. Locate such a relative and inquire about old letters. and forms relatives might have given them for safe keeping.

Old, faded papers can provide an abundance of information. Look in attics and cellars of family dwellings. Do not overlook pieces of paper stuck in corners.

A friend found a ticket stub to a concert years ago. The ticket was wedged between pieces of wood in her attic. Admission price was ninety cents to see a well known star. That single piece of paper provided a wealth of information. The house is owned by the same family.

Whoever resided in the house in 1917 liked entertainment - singing. Plus, another important point, 1917, the United States became involved in World War I. So during wartime, citizens still found time to relax.

OLD TRUNKS AND HAND BAGS

Old dusty trunks, besides having unique designs, also hold unique hiding places. Don't forget to search the lining of old hand bags and trunks. If a seam appears tampered with, maybe some glimmer of information is stored inside. If nothing else, you can get an idea of the person's style, personality type, or character from the information you gather. This kind of information is also important. It allows you to become acquainted with a long ago relative.

OTHER SOURCES

Old Photos

Have you noticed that each period of time carries with it a style, not only in clothes, but in every facet of life and living including poses for pictures? If you find old photographs and can identify the people, look at the way they are posed; also, look at the background. Was the picture black and white or in color? How was the hair styled? What was in the background? Was a familiar building present? Or did the studio use a back drop that represents the time?

Some old photos were developed on paper that is easily identified. A photographer or photography historian may be able to identify it for you. If the studio listed its name, review city records for years the studio existed. Maybe it is still around and someone can provide needed information.

Certificates

Do not forget to check your local courthouse for birth and death certificates. In some areas, midwives delivered babies, and posted birth records the day after a birth. They filed birth certificates in the same manner. If discrepancies exist in birthdates, the local courthouse can confirm if late posting of births was a practice.

Neighbors

The last source in this section is neighbors. If your family members live in the same location, do not forget neighbors as sources of valuable information. Ask for photos. Do not be disappointed, depending on the period of time and location, taking a picture was an infrequent occurrence.

Ask about relationships. Maybe someone recalls that a member of your family was a close friend of a relative.

OCCUPATIONS

Find out your relatives means of employment. This

information will tell you how your family has progressed. It will show also if your family leans toward particular professions. Here is an example: Your great grandmother was a good seamstress, your great grandfather repaired machines especially sewing machines, you are a fashion designer and your son and daughter want to be engineers. See the connection? As time passed, your family members have simply elaborated on past occupations.

IMPORTANT POINTS:

1. Organize, organize and then organize some more. This habit will save you a lot of time later when you pull all of this information together.

2. Do not interpret information. Your interpretation may add a different and incorrect slant.

3. Do not be surprised when you discover a different spelling for your own surname. Many families shortened names and changed spellings according to the region.

4. Include nicknames and maiden names along with birth and marriage names.

5. Interview all older relatives as possible sources. Do not overlook any one because the person may not appear to be a likely resource. A fact remains, most elderly persons have a better recollection of remote events than recent.

NOTES:

_____

_____

_____

_____

_____

_____

_____

_____

_____

_____

_____

_____

_____

_____

C H A P T E R

NINE:

Where To Find Information

Now that you have established some kind of workable system for storing and retrieving information, it is now time to elaborate on finding what you need to complete a family history. Many methods exist for obtaining information; however, always remember that the best method is in-person interviews. Sometimes, though, in person interviews are absolutely impossible. Schedules will conflict, the person may be timid, or the interview is not high priority at the time. Proceed with whatever resources and persons available to you, additional information will surface.

STEP ONE - PLANS FOR ORAL INTERVIEWS

Oral or in-person, both terms describe a formal or informal method of obtaining information from a person during a special conversation. Basically, this method of obtaining information requires that you have preplanned topics to discuss with relatives in a relaxed atmosphere.

Just as a researcher would ask when conducting a study, ask if it is permissible for you to tape record the interview. Establish quickly that you want to learn from the person. Let them know how important it is to record your family's history and that they are essential to this process. Do not over do it. When you finish, the person will feel proud to have been asked. Most of the time, you will know the people you interview well. Your grandparents, aunts and uncles are examples, so be very relaxed but keep them focused. These relatives will usually appreciate what you want to accomplish.

This is not the time to be someone you are not - a master interviewer, a renown television celebrity. Even if you are, remember you are with family and not at work. This approach hinders smooth communication of information. If it is okay, turn on the tape recorder and forget that it exists.

Focus your attention on the person and what is being shared. When the person pauses during conversation for an extended period, do not become annoyed or anxious.

Active listening and patience are essential virtues of interviewers. Provide reminders for the person, but allow the conversation to flow.

Ask questions that require more than a yes or no answer. If clarification is necessary, ask reflecting questions (repeat part of what the person said).

Do remember that you want stories, anecdotes and facts regarding past events. So questions you ask are crucial.

QUESTIONS TO ASK

Adjust your line of questioning to the person. For instance, if a person talks a lot, listen, record what is said, amd take a few notes. Ask for clarification only when absolutely necessary, especially when the person does not ramble or go off on tangents and is coherent. Also, do not interrupt if the person does not follow your pre-set format. You can actually destroy an opportunity to capture valuable family history if you interrupt. Imagine being engrossed in conversation and someone stops you. It is possible to forget your thoughts.

Wouldn't it be a nice bit of news to discover that your great grandmother enjoyed evening walks just as you enjoy jogging in the park in the evening. Or that you nibble on your bread the same as your great Aunt had done. Ask questions that get you this kind of information.

Additionally, ask questions that allow you to discover attitudes, ambitions, goals, personalities and hobbies. After all, you want to discover relationships. Lets suppose that you have been accused of being a fanatic when it comes to some trait or habit. Also, you have wondered about this habit. In talking with older relatives, you will probably discover that this same habit was a habit of other relatives of strong character.

Ask questions about home life. Were your relatives work-a-holics or did they hardly work. What did the children do during the day? Did they attend school? What was the highest grade level completed? Was college a consideration? If you discover that a relative attended college decades ago, this achievement was a monumental fete when you consider that colleges were few in number, money was scarce for most of the population, especially during depression years, and college degrees were not commonplace as they are today.

What about religious affiliations? Were your relatives active members? Did the family suddenly switch from one denomination or did a split occur within their place of worship?

After the interview, do not save information gathered for future review. *Summarize the material immediately*. Some of it will not make sense when you translate your notes later. Write down what was gained from the interview. Did the person mention someone else that might be a valuable resource? If so, and if it is feasible, interview them as well.

EQUIPMENT

A story of unsuspected grief is appropriate to share at this point. Read this carefully, if you have not participated in interviews before, it is essential that you purchase high quality cassette tapes.

During the midst of data collection for a study, I decided that it was time to save money. I was certain this could be accomplished by purchasing inexpensive cassette tapes. Wrong, I will never do that again. I saved money and lost an opportunity to record a conversation with a subject (person) who shared very sensitive facets of lived experiences. As these events unfolded, the subject was in tears because of a devastating experience. Suddenly a piercing noise erupted from the tape recorder. I stopped the recorder, opened the face of it to see what had caused the noise and the plastic tape exploded from the recorder. Save yourself this kind of agony and skimp on lunch but not on batteries and cassette tapes.

ENVIRONMENT

Do not become alarmed by the degree of background noise. None of us live in sound proof houses; actually, some are more sound proof than others. During a short period of time, I conducted several interviews in homes, offices, parks and other locations. Some persons lived near highways, parks, schools, mills, noisy neighborhoods and quiet neighborhoods.

Noise producing items in a home can be eliminated: television, washer, dryer, stereo, clock, telephone, radio, people, children (sometimes). However, activities outside the home are beyond your control. Allow the interview to flow. On a good day, with an expensive tape recorder and high quality tapes, I recorded a conversation, and noise from a nearby park is very audible. What can you do? Absolutely nothing. Most of the time, your interview is still quite clear. Actually noise can add character.

OTHER METHODS

Lets suppose someone identifies a person as a good resource, and it is absolutely impossible for either of you to travel to a central location. There are still ways to collect information.

Recorded Phone Conversation

Call the person long distance and explain your dilemma. Pre-arrange a time when you can call again to ask questions. Once the person has agreed to a date, you must make certain that you keep that date and time available for the call. There is a way to record the conversation. If you have two telephones, place one in a bathroom or closet with your tape recorder and cassette in place. Make sure no one uses that bathroom or closet.

Contact the person for the interview, let them know that you are recording the conversation, go to the bathroom or closet (if you have small children, traffic and one toilet). Place the headphone on top of the recorder. Turn the volume as high as it will go and start the recorder.

Begin your conversation, take notes, listen for a *click* when the tape stops. At that time tell the person to hold on for a moment while you turn the tape over. If you do not trust hearing a click, set a timer just before the cassette is due to stop. When the timer goes off, turn the tape. The purpose of using a bathroom or closet (closet works better) is to reduce extraneous noise.

Another method is designed to reduce outside noise. However, years ago (I won't say how many), when I tried this kind of gadget, it did not work. Fortunately, technology always makes up for deficits. Surely, improvements have been made over the years. Maybe the design and function have improved also.

You can purchase a gadget from a music technology store that attaches to your telephone and directly to a recorder. I know of two types: 1. attaches to the earphone by suction (did not work for me years ago) and 2. actually screws onto the speaker.

Questionnaire

If you have a relative who is inaccessible by phone (nursing home) and is coherent, ask another relative to visit that person and complete the questionnaire. If you know the relative well, and the person is willing, have the conversation recorded. If this is not possible, the information recorded on the questionnaire will be invaluable.

You can prepare a questionnaire based on the information you obtain from other in-person interviews. Suppose you have interviewed four relatives and each one talks about hobbies, religious activities, and cooking. You can then design a questionnaire with similar questions to send to relatives who have been identified as fantastic resources. Examples: What were your hobbies when you were growing up? What chores were you assigned as a child? What were your feelings when your father died? What happened to the family after his death? Be creative, some questions will be answered others will not. What year did the family stop farming? When did Uncle John marry

Aunt Mary?

Letter

Do not overlook the possibilities of a letter. Some older people, because of failing eyesight, do not like to write. Others will prefer writing over the illogical and expensive phone call. Remember the influence of depression years on older relatives' philosophy of spending (wasting) money.

Whatever method you choose to collect information, be consistent. As soon as you complete an interview, receive a questionnaire or letter, review it and record important information in your file.

FAMILY THEME

As you collect information, listen for repetitions: values, adages, attitudes, beliefs and philosophies. Did similarities transcend generations? Commonalities and similarities could be value judgments, approaches to ethical behavior, political involvement, methods of childrearing, or utilization of money. If so, a pattern or trend exists within your family line. Think of what you discover and write it down.

Try to visualize family members for a moment. What behaviors dominate? Are they the same or similar to behaviors exhibited during years gone by? Try to summarize that "sameness" into a brief paragraph. This sameness becomes your family's theme or philosophy.

There is yet another way of discovering your family's theme. It is amazing how much we are alike as humans and even more so when we are with our families. This information is obtained during your reunion. It is then that members of a family line discover their sameness.

During your reunion's business meeting, provide each family member, who is able to write, a piece of paper, hopefully everyone will have a pen or pencil. Have pens on hand just in case. Ask these or similar questions. What values are most important to you? What does family mean? What does hard work accomplish for you? Explain future plans. Basically, after collecting all of this information you want to find out how each person relates to the other philosophically.

Some people will complete all of the questions others will not. Review responses. You will work with completed responses first. Since you are not conducting scientific research, use the incomplete statements when a complete response is included. Keep others in a pile or in back of the completed ones.

The responses to these questions will be short. Look for buzz words. Start with question one. Write all repeat terms down. Do the same for all questions. Assess the terms or buzz words in question one. Is there anything significant listed? Look at the example below:

1. What values are most important to you? Honesty, responsibility, truth, fairness, justice, loyalty
    Four of the terms listed indicate that most family members in the example value honesty. All terms relate to this one word. Therefore, in writing the family's theme utilizing this word, a sentence would either include the one term or additional

related terms.

> The Kay family values honesty
> in their everyday existence. Each person
> seeks honesty, fairness, and justice as
> they relate to the world.

An even shorter version of the above example could be - The Kay Family, *relating to the world in honesty, truth and justice.* When would you even need or want to write a family theme? Whenever and wherever you desire. Print it on family tee-shirts, mugs, stationery, brochures and as a way to reach young, troubled members of your family.

People tend to live their lives according to expectations. Using the Kay's family theme, the following expectation surfaces: A cashier gave you $10.00 too much, what do you do? Remember honesty, fairness, truth, justice. The answer is simple, return the money.

Once a large percentage of your group approves the theme, incorporate it in all that you do. Revise it often, or keep it in its original form. If you do revise it, get suggestions from family members. You can then start a conversation when a non-family member asks about it.

IMPORTANT POINTS:

1. *Be open minded when pursuing information. Investigate all possible resources.*
2. *Somehow, keep records of information sources.*
3. *Revere older members of your family. Teach your children to do the same. Treasure the history that exists within their lived experiences. They are eager to share.*
4. *Your family's theme can represent your values and distinguish you*

from other families.

NOTES:

_____

_____

_____

_____

_____

_____

_____

_____

_____

_____

_____

_____

_____

_____

_____

NOTES:

The generations of living things pass in a short time, and like runners hand on the torch of life. -**Lucretias,** *De Rerum Natura*

C H A P T E R

TEN:

Genealogy

This chapter provides information for your family's background search. Genealogy, in fact, is the scientific study of family history. Information is discovered on births, marriages, divorces, and deaths. The information is arranged on a pedus or pedigree, commonly called a family tree.

Tracing your history is a fascinating and sometimes frustrating endeavor. Regardless of your ancestry, much of your family's past is recoverable. As you piece puzzles together and become a self-assigned detective, family mysteries unfold. Your adventure will be exciting. Spread the thrill throughout your family line.

Entire texts and even libraries are devoted to this topic. Information included here provides an introduction to resources available to you when researching your family line, tree, roots or pedigree.

It is important that you review chapters eight and nine: methods of obtaining information and where to find it. In this chapter, however, more specific information is retrieved from sources other than relatives. Unless, of course, relatives have copies of certificates, marriage licenses, military papers and other significant documents.

At first, it will seem as though information included in this chapter should be easy to locate. For this generation it is. However, when you *step* back in time, retrieval of history is not so easy, especially when the realization pops out at you that records of life events do not exist.

RULES

Before you begin your search, become familiar with commonly held rules for this section. Five main ones are:

1. develop a good record-keeping system
2. begin your investigation with yourself and work back one ancestor at a time
3. search each and every record and not just a portion of them
4. be extremely accurate in recording all facts
5. do not paraphrase information or correct spelling

The first person to investigate when preparing your genealogy is you. Respond to questions you plan to ask others. If information retrieval does not work for you with the system you plan to employ, then it will not work for others.

Appendix G contains a form that will make this part easier: *Personal History Information Sheet.* It is an easy fill-in-the-blank form. Start with your family of origin and record this kind of information for all family members. If relatives are willing to assist you, get them to use the information sheet.

When the information collected according to the *Personal History Information Sheet* becomes difficult for you, this same section may be difficult for your relatives. At that point, it is time to seek answers from other sources. This chapter will include important points to aid in completing your search from sources outside the family: county records, local libraries, census reports, genealogical collections, and federal records.

COUNTY RECORDS

Before you contact a county records office, make sure that your initial family search is thorough. Obtaining copies of documents from a county records office can be expensive, especially if you request copies in several cities.

County records offices have copies of birth, marriage, death, and divorce certificates. Any county records office will have addresses for locations in other cities. Write a letter or telephone and request documents. Most offices will not mail requested information without appropriate fees.

An important point to remember in your search is that many counties have been divided or merged. Some records are non-existent because of damage by a flood or fire. Sometimes, non-existent records is due to carelessness.

When you write to any office include the persons' name, event date, residence, names of other relatives, and fee. If the fee you include is not correct, a clerk will notify you by mail. What happens when the information needed for a clerk to search for a document is the exact information you do not have? Provide the information you do have and an approximate date of the event. In many counties, a clerk will conduct a search within a few years of that date.

LOCAL LIBRARIES

All public libraries have information on genealogy. Do not assume because a library is small that it is not possible to find assistance. Contact the librarian. Many librarians will go out of their way to assist you. Find a book on county history, genealogy, and surnames. The librarian will suggest other titles from the library's holdings. Some public libraries maintain family biographies and support exchanges between families.

My experience with a local library was very positive. The librarian provided an eight page document to assist in my personal search. Once the preliminary information is complete, the librarian begins a search through numerous county records on microfiche. So, do not despair if you have not been successful on your own.

CENSUS RECORDS

Census records are housed in the National Archives in Washington, D.C. on microfilm. A librarian can request a copy of a microfilm on interlibrary loan. In addition, Federal Archives are located in major cities throughout the country. These branches house census records for specific geographic regions.

The first census in the United States was completed in 1790. You can have access to all census tracks from 1790 to 1900. After that time, access is restricted. To obtain information, you must submit a request in writing. Information is only supplied for the person making the request. If information is needed for a deceased person, you must include a copy of the death certificate.

When the idea of a census was something new, most people did not tell the census-taker the truth. Most people thought census takers were tax agents or just plain nosey. Census-takers did not expect the truth. People lied about their ages and number of persons in a dwelling. Some census takers could not spell; others did not take their jobs seriously.

You must prepare yourself when you are ready to use the census as a source of information. It is best to search reports that are available to you. Census reports taken in 1790 are very limited (Table 1). Listings are by county, the number of free persons in a household, and the number of slaves.

The census of 1880 marks the onset of detailed information. Census of 1890 was destroyed by fire, only a few records exist. No information is included in the 1870 census on slaves. The 1900 census should prove to be very valuable. Most people get excited when they have access to

TABLE 1-Comparison of Census Data 1790-1810/1900

	1790	1800	1810	1900
1. Name of head of family	x	x	x	x
2. Number of free white males	x	x	x	
3. Number of free white females	x	x	x	
4. Place of residence	x	x	x	x
5. Number of foreigners not naturalized				x
6. Name of each family member				x
7. Age of each family member				x
8. Month and year of birth				x
9. Sex of each family member				x
10. Whether attended school				x
11. Whether read or write				x
12. Relationship to head of family				x
13. Marital status				x
14. Birthplace of mother and father				x
15. Number of months unemployed within year				x
16. Occupation				x
17. Color of each family member				x
18. Number of years married				x
19. Mother of how many children				x
20. How many living children				x
21. Year of immigration to U.S.				x
22. Whether speak English				x
23. Ownership of home				x

Please note the increase in information collected for the census in 1900. Retrieval of this information provides quite a bit of history for your family.

their past through census reports, especially for this particular decade. This resource will add a sense of connectedness to your past. The infinite amount of time spent searching for completeness in your family's records is well invested.

GENEALOGICAL COLLECTIONS

No book on family reunions and genealogy can exclude mentioning the popular work of Alex Haley, *Roots* or of Marilyn Heimberg, *Discover Your Roots*. It was in a library that Haley realized the possibility of a book.

The largest collection of genealogical information is owned by the Latter Day Saints in Salt Lake City, Utah. Others exist but their holdings do not compare. The collection in Salt Lake City started out of a need for affiliates of the church to know their ancestors' histories.

The next largest private collection is housed in Chicago, the Newberry Collection. The Newberry Collection has information on people residing in all regions of the U. S.; however, the collection's holdings center on the mid-west.

A minor fee is accessed for information retrieved from genealogical collections. Send a letter to: *The Newberry Library, 60 West Walton Street, Chicago, Illinois 60610.*

FEDERAL RECORDS

An abundance of information exists in the National Archives in Washington. If your leads have not proven true for collecting information, you are destined to be successful with your efforts at the National Archives.

But who can travel to Washington just to seek information. Not many people can or want to do that. Several regional branches are located throughout the country. Area branches are listed here:

1. Los Angeles Federal Archives and Records Center
   24000 Avila Road
   Laguna Niguel, California 92677
   Records for: Arizona, Southern California, and parts of
   Nevada

2. San Francisco Federal Archives and Records Center
   1000 Commodore Drive
   San Bruno, California 94066
   Records For: North California, Hawaii, Nevada, Pacific
   territory, American Somoa

3. Denver Federal Archives and Records Center
   Building 48, Denver Federal Center
   Denver, Colorado 80225
   Records for: Colorado, Montana, North and South
   Dakota, Utah, and Wyoming

4. Atlanta Federal Archives and Records Center
   1557 St. Joseph Avenue
   East Point, Georgia 30344
   Records for: Georgia, Alabama, Florida, Kentucky,
   Mississippi, North and South Carolina, and
   Tennessee

5. Chicago Federal Archives and Records Center
   7358 South Pulaski Road
   Chicago, Illinois 60629
   Records for: Illinois, Indiana, Michigan, Minnesota,
   Ohio, and Wisconsin

6. Boston Federal Archives and Records Center
   380 Trapelo Road
   Waltham, Massachusetts 02154
Records for: Massachusetts, Connecticut, Maine, New
                      Hampshire, Rhode Island, and Vermont

7. Kansas City Federal Archives and Records Center
   2306 East Bannister Road
   Kansas City, Missouri 64131
Records for: Kansas, Iowa, Missouri, and Nebraska

8. New York Federal Archives and Records Center
   Building 22-MOT Bayonne
   Bayonne, New Jersey 07002
Records for: New Jersey, New York, Puerto Rico, and Virgin
                      Islands

9. Philadelphia Federal Archives and Records Center
   5000 Wissahickon Avenue
   Philadelphia, Pennsylvania 19144
Records for: Pennsylvania, Delaware, District of Columbia,
                      Maryland, Virginia, and West Virginia

10. Fort Worth Federal Archives and Records Center
    4900 Hemphill Street
    Ft Worth, Texas 76115
Records for: Texas, Arkansas, Louisiana, New Mexico, Oklahoma

11. Seattle Federal Archives and Records Center
    6125 Sand Point Way NE
    Seattle, Washington 98115
Records for: Washington, Idaho, Oregon, and Alaska

Librarians in each archive will respond to inquiries if sufficient information is included. Do not give up if your search is not successful. Write to the National Archive in Washington, D.C. for additional assistance.

OTHER RESOURCES

The Library of Congress is another source of family genealogical information. It has the largest collection of family history in the U.S., over 30,000 volumes. It also has some 90,000 titles that focus on American history.

When you discover the dates your ancestors lived, librarians and publications can assist you to imagine their life. Style of clothes, tools, food, handwriting, songs, history itself will provide vivid pictures of lifestyles.

Military status of family members can provide a different dimension to your family's history. If the person's unit, regiment, company or ship or other information is known include it with your request. To aid your search send for a copy of a free pamphlet, "Military Service Records in the National Archives of the United States."

When you discover your relatives' occupations and accomplishments, you have to divorce yourself of twentieth century thought. You cannot judge an occupation during the 1800s by any other period of time except 1800s. Most women were housewives. Anything other than teaching and delivering babies was unthinkable.

No, this is not a history lesson. However, it is a reminder for you to respect the occupations, or lack there of, during your investigation. Occupations for women simply did not exist during certain periods of time. The definition of *normal* changes with each generation and certainly with periods of time. At some point in the future, regardless of how much progress women have made, someone will view our present occupations with total disdain. So be careful.

IMPORTANT POINTS:

1. *Establish a record keeping system, begin your investigation with your family of origin, search all available records, record all facts, and do not make corrections or paraphrase information you find.*
2. *Complete the Personal History Information Sheet (Appendix G).*
3. *When researching additional sources, list census records as a possible resource. Start with the 1900 census and work back a generation at a time.*
4. *Contact the Federal Archive and Records Center in your region.*

NOTES:

PART III
Investing In Your Family's Future

I believe the power to make money is a gift of God. -**John D. Rockefeller, quoted in** *The Robber Barons*

C
H
A
P
T
E
R

ELEVEN:

Your Family's Future

Just why did I include this section? Because investing money should be a primary topic for families and not just individuals. What better place to start than at a reunion when a majority of all family members are present. Just think of the many ways to approach this topic: a speaker, column in the family newsletter, distribution of a flyer.

I mentioned earlier that each family in the United States has members who are experts on numerous topics. Why not capitalize on that expertise. Right now, do you have money sitting in a savings account? Or worse yet, do you simply deposit all incoming cash into your checking account and allow it to accumulate? That extra money can make money for essential purchases and investments.

PERSONAL EXPERIENCE

A personal experience will emphasize my point. I put money in a certificate of deposit and left it there for five years. The original transaction was for one year. When I decided to cash it in, I was penalized part of the already low interest earned for making the transaction one day after the money had been reinvested. How is this a horror story? Read on, you will find out.

U. S. News and World Report includes an annual segment on investing, usually in its January issue. It was there that I received confirmation of investing money wisely. If you have money that you can put into a reserve without using it for normal household operation, and to get the most for your dollar, it is best to invest it some way but not a savings account or CD, if, money growth is a goal. If I had invested half of the original amount in a mutual fund, after five years, I would have received more than what I invested. To me, to collect far less after five years, when I think of the alternative method of *growing* money, is a horror story.

It is difficult to think of the future of your family without wondering about economics. Educational expenses are prohibitive at some private institutions. State supported schools increase their tuition and fees annually as well. Transportation to family functions is expensive when you consider the overall aspect of economics.

When you stop and think for a moment, researching family history leads to a sense of belonging and closeness. A result of this new feeling within the family is a trend toward scheduling additional meetings. The cycle continues.

Back to economics for your family. I did not just throw these paragraphs in to fill up space. As your meetings continue, love for your family increases, concern for them increases as well.

Why not do something about those feelings of closeness. Family meetings are wonderful. Don't get me wrong, I enjoy my relatives. I discover relationships each time we meet. I believe positive ventures could start from family meetings.

Many talented people come from the same family, most trust each other implicitly. Some even get advice on business ventures from trusted family members after being cheated by an unrelated, and not so well known partner.

With the state of the economy today and with a glimmer of hope of change, why not take hold of family knowledge as well. If this sort of maneuver appeals to you, read further. If not, reread this section later. Maybe your hesitation is because you lack experience in investing and in business. Venture out, think big, expand.

FAMILY INVENTORY

Since you are still reading, finances must be of interest to you. The absolute first thing you must do is take an inventory of your family. Write down names of close relatives. List positive attributes. What are their occupations, hobbies, interests, strong points, recent ideas shared, aspirations? Write all of this down. Simplify this part, review copies of Appendix F that your relatives completed (*Family Inventory*).

You are on a roll and must have something in mind if you put this book down to get a paper and pencil. Some of the richest people in the world have entered into ventures with other relatives. Siblings, cousins, aunts, uncles, parents, grandparents, nieces and nephews, the combination is endless. Don't overlook anyone.

The one combination I want to share with you now involves your entire family. What in the world could I possibly have in mind. Read on, it does get interesting.

As the year 2000 approaches, it is a very sane strategy for families to consider how economics will affect them as a unit instead of how economics will affect each part. The former kind of thinking is call systems theory. A family can function together like a well oiled machine. Each member or part completing its task to make a whole.

TIPS FOR INVESTORS

Before you consider any of the ideas shared in this chapter, or others to enhance your family's future, read these *tips* and obtain advice from an investment consultant:

1. Research the company or mode of investing before you do so
2. Know the company's history or that of your agent
3. How does the company fair with its competitor
4. Diversify into several stock options (not all will do well)

5. A good company will increase its dividends every year
6. Do not select a stock because it is inexpensive
7. Beware that a stock can bottom, at that point it can go lower
8. Tips I have received suggest that investing in small prosperous companies is best (contact your investment agent)
9. Stocks tend to do better that bonds
10. Stocks and mutual funds perform better than bonds, CDs and money-market funds.
11. Higher yield with stocks

JOINT EDUCATIONAL INVESTMENT

The idea proposed here could end as a small project or escalate into a mammoth undertaking. Lets suppose your family consists of 100 relatives from grandparents to cousins. In that combination of relations, four are babies and six are in elementary school and seven are in junior high. From the total of 17 children, a large percentage will attend college, vocational school or other form of extended educational training.

The cost of education is tremendous today. By the year 2015, the cost of education is expected to skyrocket. The monumental increase that is anticipated would receive little attention if jobs and salaries also kept pace with this expenditure. This parallel spiral would be nice but not likely.

Why not purchase stock, mutual funds, and municipal and treasury bonds, or some kind of certificate as a family venture that will mature in time for each group of children to attend college. It would be a welcomed experience for each child's parents to receive a check from the family's educational foundation at the dawn of college.

Who is retired in your family? Someone who is organized and a self-starter. Someone who would welcome an opportunity to establish a foundation for the family. Think about it, let this idea grow on you.

How does it work? It is not as difficult as it sounds. There are two ways to establish this family project. First, introduce the idea at your next family reunion. Provide each person with a copy of the idea proposed here or your own.

I do know that some family members have the capability of swindling the church choir if given the opportunity. At least you know about them. I am not suggesting that you give these relatives your grocery money, let alone your life savings or even a portion of it. I am merely suggesting that after attending several family reunions, you realize that people of strong character and intellectual ability are your relatives.

In some circles, these same people you grew up with and know embarrassing tails about are movers and shakers. Capitalize on their knowledge and abilities.

Suggest having a speaker at each reunion that will benefit the entire family. Presentations can be on self-improvement, economics, business, finance, health, and travel. After all, haven't you heard the old stories before. Discuss a topic with a new twist - investing.

Method One - Foundation

Get each family member to contribute the exact same amount of money to the non-profit foundation. Doesn't that make your contribution tax deductible? Yes, it does. With yearly dividends, you also will offer a competitive scholarship to a non-relative. You get my point? People who have children will welcome the idea and people without children or whose children are out of college will welcome the opportunity to help family members. Plus, there is that added incentive of a tax deduction.

Method Two - Percentages

Offer the idea in the same way; however, this time offer available percentages. Say you want to invest $10-25,000.00 in low risk minimum yield stock. Relatives will then have an opportunity to purchase a part of the total amount. When the stock or other investment matures, or when it is time to trade or sell, each investor's portion is the original percentage invested of the matured amount.

If I invest 20% of $20,000, invested wisely, the matured amount could be several times the original amount. For the sake of realism, I could live with any amount over my original investment.

For some, my example requires entirely too much time. Five years is a long time. Here is another example. Lets suppose the same amount is invested for one or two years. In some markets, the invested amount doubles and even triples. Again, I could live with a portion of the return.

SAME IDEA, DIFFERENT STRATEGY - A FEW INVESTORS - Monthly

Okay, so working with the entire family is a bit

unnerving for you. Here is another possibility. For years, you have talked with some of your siblings and cousins about investments. Most of you have solo investments already. *Get with those relatives, put your money together and form an investment club!* The invested amount could be as small as $25.00 a month, but look at the yield.

It helps that all of you are aware of investments and what is entailed. Do remember to seek legal counsel on developing a plan and regarding the division of profits. An accountant and an investment counselor can assist you. Each person files a form 1099 and must be committed to a preset maturity date.

SAME IDEA, DIFFERENT STRATEGY - DONATIONS

Here is where the idea blossoms into a mammoth undertaking. When you establish a foundation for your family, you can solicit donations. With this strategy, you might as well open a non-profit business. This kind of project requires full time attention to work as it should. You will need a license, income tax identification number, non-profit status, incorporation status, accountant, you get the picture. This idea could work for the diligent. Most important, the public must be aware of your foundation.

ANOTHER IDEA - Safe

Want to plan a reunion in an exotic location? It can be done, if you plan right away! Identify a location, Hawaii,

Las Vegas, Caribbean Islands, Europe, Asia. Use your imagination. The idea of a reunion cruise is simply SPECTACULAR!

Get with a reputable travel agent and estimate ALL costs as close to reality as possible for today's market. Ask the travel agent to project a cost two years from now, or whenever you plan this special reunion. Add the amounts together and have the total ready to present to the planning committee.

At your next reunion, get each interested person to commit to attendance by placing money in a monitored investment of some kind that matures in two years. In two years split the return among the original investors. This is a way to reduce the expense of your dream vacation/family reunion.

Investigate different forms of investments, and especially those few with *no load (service charge). What about taxes? What about administrative problems and fees? Look at your family inventory, who is your most likely person for advice? Before you jump into an idea, ask an investment accountant, cpa, or attorney for advice.*

COOKBOOK OR OTHER SPECIAL PROJECT

Here is yet another *safe* idea that carries low risk for your entire family. Children can get involved, too. In fact, whatever you do design a section *called For Kids By Kids.*

Announce the idea of a family cookbook in your newsletter. Since everyone will benefit from the proceeds, encourage each person to bring or send tons of recipes.

Ask a willing soul to coordinate this activity. Once

expenses are paid, remaining money goes toward family events.

BUSINESS PARTNERS/INCORPORATION

This is my *FAVORITE SECTION,* why you ask? Because this category of investment ideas is about workable plans that not only mimic business ventures but are like any business in society with little to no risk (depending on the venture). Possibilities are endless.

Here is an example. Hypothetically, an announcement has been made through the *Federal Registry* for a nonprofit or private company to administer a program for unwed teen mothers. From the announcement, you know that you will need counselors, nurses, social workers, and contact with other resource persons. You are fortunate because your siblings and cousins are employed in these very positions.

Speak to your relatives about a partnership or corporation. Get assistance from SCORE (Service Core of Retired Employers). They are located in most large cities. The unique part about SCORE is that their services are free. Or look to the Minority Business Development League, if you qualify as an ethnic minority. Many categories are listed in their guidelines. Services offered are unbelievable for a padre $10.00 per hour.

Don't forget your local Chamber of Commerce when you need assistance. One of its primary functions is to anticipate needs of prospective businesses. If you offer a service, for example counseling, a business may need a program on stress reduction for its employees. Contact the chamber and get listed in a business directory.

Do you live near a community college or trade school?

If you do, you are in luck. Call the business school. Sometimes you can get information or have the school adopt your idea for a project.

With an incorporated business, all of you are investors and possible employees. If done properly, this idea could be an investment that pays off more than you could ever imagine. Get a license, *incorporate*, apply for non-profit status (if applicable), call IRS for a tax-ID number (have to submit application by mail later), and find a reputable accountant.

FAMILY GRADUATION FUND

Does your family have children who will graduate from high school soon? If not soon, eventually you will. Pool funds to provide each graduate with a book scholarship or gift from the family. Don't wait for other agencies to supply your needs. Provide for your family's youth now.

KIDS' BANK

A child cannot progress to adulthood and suddenly know everything there is to know about investing and spending money wisely when opportunities to make money-wise decisions have not existed. *Most parents perpetuate the myth of the money tree.*

Open a family kids' bank. Invest money for each child. To do this, each child must have a social security number. Keep a roster of investors. Allow children to serve as board members (elected by their peers). Chairperson should be an adult family member. During your reunion is an excellent time for each child to review their file for money deposited and interest earned. Discuss plans for new ventures and vote on ideas from members.

This idea adds another dimension to a reunion for everyone. Even regular savings accounts monitored during your reunion is a great idea. If money remains, divide it and make a deposit into each account. Better yet, invest a bulk sum and split dividends among your family's youth.

Now, who will monitor your funds? Again, look to your retired relatives. Select honest and organized people who were active and responsible before they retired. Again, this activity requires a lot of time (want details - coming soon to your local bookstore: *Teaching Adults and Children About the Mythical Money Tree).*

IMPORTANT POINTS:

1. *Compile the information you collected with the Family Inventory and distribute it among your relatives.*
2. *Utilize your resources, possibilities are endless.*

NOTES:

_____

_____

_____

_____

Time present and time past, are both perhaps
present in time future, and time future
contained in time past.
-T.S.Eliot, *Burnt Norton, in Four Quartets*

C
H
A
P
T
E
R

TWELVE:

Continuing The Closeness

Another surefire way to invest in your family's future is to continue the closeness. Feelings you share at reunions and other gatherings should not end when the event is over. Plan to continue that closeness you feel throughout the year. You can incorporate simple activities into your plans to facilitate communication.

First, and again, while your group is together, announce plans for pen pals, family buddies, and a newsletter. Two of these ideas are cost free and generate opportunities for relationship building and extending family strengths. Think of other methods to continue *the closeness*. The methods suggested here require additional emphasis.

PEN PALS

With this activity, selecting pen pals is not left to chance. This common method of communication requires a bit of imagination. People who have had contact with each other over the years should not have freedom to select pen pals. No, this is not a democratic activity. Most people, if given a choice, will automatically select someone they know. *Pair family members with cousins they have just met.*

Everyone can participate even relatives who claim a spontaneous onset of temporary illiteracy, arthritis, deafness, and failing eyesight. Instead of letters, send cassette tapes or make phone calls. If the aforementioned measures are not creative enough, try this one. Develop a code for communicating or communicate in a different language that both people are trying to learn.

What does "pig latin" mean to you? If family members are of the generation that were fascinated with it, suggest that people try to decode letters written this way.

Why not learn a new language or play chess or checkers through the mail. Have you been approached by a relative because of your tutoring skills? Well, it is time to expand. Why not tutor someone in a subject by mail. Opportunities are endless for continuing the closeness.

FAMILY BUDDY

Is there a family member living in a new city alone? Is someone an only child? Have you or someone else ever wanted to travel around the world or even to the next city, but you wanted someone to buddy up with? Wouldn't it be great to pair or team up with a buddy? A new family member is great.

Relationships of this nature just might start out platonic, but could result in strong family ties later. Each person has a vested interest and all have one commonality, being related. Being buddies strengthens the relatedness.

NEWSLETTER

A family of 50 has 50 or more items of news to report. When this method of continuing closeness is suggested, most relatives will deny having newsworthy information. Assure them that each person present has a headliner in their bones.

What about vacations? Where did you go? Nowhere? Still that is newsworthy:

JANE DOE SPENDS ENTIRE VACATION LOCKED IN HOME EATING ICE CREAM

Jane Doe admitted this week that she spent her entire vacation munching ice cream of all varieties. If given the opportunity again, she said, "I would do it the same way." She said that in addition to eating ice cream she slept a lot.

Jane lives in sunny Sun City. She travels on her job seven months out of each year. She is interested in hearing from other vacation potatoes. By the way, Jane reports to have gained only two pounds during her short-lived binge.

Combine appendices A-D as an example of a newsletter. Reformat it, use headers that get attention. Your newsletter can include all kinds of information. Here is another example:

AUNT MARY RAISES PRIZE TOMATOES!

Aunt Mary, who turned 90 last month, has shared with this reporter that her smallest tomato weighed 8 ounces! Way to go Aunt Mary.

Aunt Mary has raised vegetables for 60 years. This year she poured a secret potion at the base of each plant. She wants you to contact her if you want to know her secret.

SUMMARY

When your family history is written, include a progress report of relationships that have been discovered. Distant relatives soon become friends and welcome an opportunity to explore relationships.

IMPORTANT POINTS:

1. Trying to facilitate family closeness can be as enjoyable as it can be disappointing, at first.

2. Do remember that family closeness, as you discover new relationships, is a change, and for most people, change is viewed with a bit of skepticism. Establishing new relationships can be inviting and also threatening. So give these new relationships several reunions to develop.

3. Do not force relationships allow discovery to occur naturally!

NOTES:

_____

_____

_____

_____

_____

_____

_____

_____

_____

_____

_____

_____

_____

_____

_____

_____

_____

PART IV
Putting It All Together

C
H
A
P
T
E
R

THIRTEEN:

From Start To Finish

Connecting the information together that you have collected into a useable format for your family is the most exciting part of all the work you have completed. Now is the time to focus on writing a family history as well as an oral presentation when your relatives meet.

Four points are explored in this chapter: writing a family history, an oral presentation, more points for experienced reunion organizers, and finally, more points for novice organizers. The first point, writing a family history, is most exciting. The potential for a best selling novel looms in someone's hands. Don't believe me, visit your local library and discover the vast number of family histories written by ordinary people and not screen writers. Finally, results of hard work connects your family line and leads to a *spectacular reunion.*

WRITING A FAMILY HISTORY

Gather all information collected. It is time to write your family's history. You do not have to be a literary genius or a Rhodes Scholar to write.

Start with the basic idea. Why have you gone to all of this trouble? Write your reason as an introduction to the history. Usual reasons given are because you wanted to record family history, learn about your past, and communicate findings to other family members. It is just that simple.

Communication of findings brings with it a special kind of relationship within the family when you discover how similar your past is to your present. During your search, if a *character* was discovered, feature that person in your paper. Maybe the person was heroic during a war, or made peach preserves for the town, or became the neighborhood pseudo-psychiatrist. Properly poised, this information sets the stage for your presentation.

If you decide to write a family history, start as far back as your information carried you. Focus on that period of time. What was going on in the rest of the country and the world during their life time? Make a statement about those events. They had an impact on your family's lifestyle. For instance, the depression. How did your family prepare for it? What were they doing at that time? How were they employed? Or were they? Who purchased the first car? Were your family members farmers? When did they stop?

Let your thoughts flow. Write an outline first to ensure that your thoughts have form and direction. Develop a short paper and expand it later. Make sure that your paper is free of errors because in addition to distributing it to family members, you can deposit it in local libraries, historical and genealogical societies.

As you write, remember that some family histories become national best sellers. Take time to write your paper, maybe later you can write a book. Review the market and take a different approach to what has been done.

ORAL HISTORIES

An oral history is a verbal accounting of your family's life. The ideal definition would have one person serve as a family historian. Then, someone becomes the storehouse for family treasures - a *curator*.

These days, people in general discard everything within a short period of time. I predict that very soon, families will realize that some so-called junk items are very valuable for family history. It is too late for some, but numerous families can start anew.

Your reunion is a good place to start your inquiry. Ask family members about hand-me-downs: christening gowns, crocheted booties, quilts. Get them cleaned by a reputable cleaner, have the items of clothing framed. The hand-me-downs or old clothes are transformed into *precious items to discuss that have visual appeal.*

EXPERIENCED REUNION ORGANIZERS

The first section of this manual discussed organizing a family reunion. If reunions, in some form, are held for your family, at the next one suggest that you and a committee of volunteers investigate your family's history (or add to an existing history). Share information with others that is included here. Tasks ahead are not so complex for you since reunions are already established.

The possibility also exists that your family's history has been investigated and fine tuned as well. Request to feature someone from the past. Complete a thorough search of the person's occupation, religious affiliation, personality, education, hobbies, and other topics.

Wealthy and gregarious family members are often familiar personalities. What about a relative who was not so colorful? If you are planning your first or even your fifty-first reunion, there is still something new to share with family members.

NOVICE REUNION ORGANIZERS

On the other hand, if reunions are not held for your family, getting relatives to that point is often difficult. But do not despair. Even in well established families, where family reunions are well organized, rest assured, someone had a difficult time getting the family to that point.

Just remember, it is rare to have 100% participation on your first or 21st. Always celebrate any number of relatives that gather, even 10% or less. The next year, watch, your number will increase, and even more so in the future.

Now that you have read through this manual, go back to the section that is most appropriate for you. Make copious notes, and write an outline of activities.

SUMMARY

At this point, writing the history and preparing an oral presentation is similar to saving your dessert for later in the day. You are finally able to breathe a sigh of relief and enjoy the pleasure. Whatever style of writing you employ, keep your information logical, and non-threatening.

Seasoned organizers and novices will reap the same benefit in the end - opportunities to discover relationships.

IMPORTANT POINTS:

1. *Organize your material in piles as you sort through it. Have a pen and paper handy. The most emphasized point becomes a heading.*
2. *Keep a tape recorder handy.*
3. *Make an outline for all activities.*
4. *Set aside time to write, honor it, and write. The project's end will come.*

NOTES:

The past is the present, isn't it? It's the future, too.
-Eugene O'Neill, *Long Day's Journey Into Night*

E P I L O G U E

The Future

Get excited about your family. Entertain each other. Enjoy your moments together and maximize your family's potential. When you discover relationships, your family's history, theme, and vision connect you in a special way.

A family reunion provides the forum for relatives to gather and renew acquaintances and to strengthen family ties. A spectacular reunion provides the stimulus for going forth with relationships to develop everyday connections.

Family history is a focal point for any reunion, and, so is its future - its youth. Handing over the torch, the family name and history, to its youth continues the integrity of the family line.

All activities included are designed to assist you to plan a SPECTACULAR family reunion. Every event has a beginning and an ending. Start now to discover your heritage and put an end to evasiveness, confusion and myths.

Like a ball that gains momentum and moves along a trajectory, a reunion propels your family toward infinite possibilities - through newly discovered relationships.

GET EXCITED - GET BUSY

HAVE FUN, AND ENJOY EACH OTHER!

Let me hear from you.

APPENDIX A:

INVITATION FROM CHAIR OF THE SMITH FAMILY REUNION

A hearty hello from Union City all descendants of Mary Smith. Our number is huge and our lifestyles are varied. We, the Smith family, live and have traveled to numerous places in the world. Lets continue our efforts to get to know each other. We are unique as individuals and even more so as a group. Lets plan to share our backgrounds with each other during Reunion 1993.

We are a talented and versatile group: athletic, innovative, intelligent, risk-takers, outgoing, flexible, caring and sharing; we need to know about each other. The meaning of FAMILY REUNION should and MUST mean more than going to a city to laugh and eat with people you do not really know. It should mean strength and support.

During this planning time, we will have area coordinators. These people are challenged to make contact with each and every family member within their area to stimulate interest and to ensure that in 1993, attendance will surpass all others. We want each and every person to attend. When the fee is tabulated, please send in what you can between April and before June 1993. You will receive a computer printout of the amount paid in your registration package; and, you will receive a copy of the Committee's Financial Report during our business meeting.

I have enjoyed meeting my relatives, and as chairperson for 1993, I intend to follow in my predecessors' footsteps and maximize our time together. Please come one, come all, to the Smith Family's 10th Reunion.

Respectfully and lovingly submitted,

APPENDIX B:

SUMMARY OF MID-YEAR PLANNING MEETING

The Smith Family's Reunion Planning Committee met at the home of the 1993 Reunion Committee's Chairperson Ann Tate. Area coordinators are:

1. Alabama -
2. Colorado -
3. Florida -
4. Georgia -
5. Michigan -
6. Kentucky -

Also in attendance:
Kim Ray
Francis Keath
Now on to the business at hand.

****

Ann distributed a meeting agenda, information flyer, brochure of proposed activities available in the Columbus area and a reunion folder. First item on the agenda, definite dates:

REUNION DATES FOR 1993, 7/29-8/1

Please make a note of these very important dates!

APPENDIX C:

ITINERARY AND ANNOUNCEMENTS

First Day

    REUNION REGISTRATION is scheduled for July 28,1993 at Hotel Tops at 5:00pm - 7:00pm. You are encouraged to register between these hours so you will be ready for the "Get Acquainted Session": 7:30pm. Prizes will be announced at 7:45pm, and you must be present to win. Tickets will be placed in registration packs; each person attending Reunion 1993 will receive a registration pack (registration fees are essential to pay for activities-everyone must pay).

Second Day

    BREAKFAST-location undecided, time is approximately 7:30am, followed by a bus tour of interesting facilities around 9:30am: A box lunch will be served enroute.
    TENTATIVE FREE TIME 4:00pm to 6:30pm
    7:00pm (approximately) an INDOOR BAR-BE-CUE (local restaurant) or FISH FRY IN a park.
    A BUSINESS MEETING will follow immediately after the bar-be-cue or fish fry.

Third Day

    FUN WALK/RUN APPROXIMATELY 7:00 to 9:00am prizes given for age category winners (all walkers and runners are encouraged to wear their reunion tee-shirt [in every registration pack]).
    BREAKFAST tentatively scheduled for 9:30 to 11:30am
    TENTATIVE FREE TIME 11:30am to 3:00pm
    OPTIONAL SIDE TOURS-3:00pm to 5:00pm or during free time-Gofer Fun Park for children and shopping for adults.

***ANNOUNNING THE BIGGEY FOR REUNION 1993 -- DRUM ROLL PLEASE!!

7:00pm Talent Show-Dinner Banquet-Dance, catered by Duck Soup, on July 29, 1993. Area coordinators were asked to inform people in their areas to forward any talent they would like to share, one per household, please. Can you sing, or not sing but you feel moved to share your voice with us anyway (I feel an urge a coming), play an instrument, tell a good joke, dance, WHATEVER, sign up now by sending in your talent and musical accompaniment title (no duplications allowed please-so be first). I need this information by March 1, 1993. Whether you are six MONTHS or 60 YEARS; you can be in the show.

Fourth Day

8:00am until 10:00am BREAKFAST (ON YOUR OWN)
11:00am - We want to encourage all family members to attend worship services at Gethsemane Baptist Church, 11:00am. Let's say farewell in unison by sharing service together. However, other places of worship will be included in your registration packs.

ANNOUNCEMENT ONE:

ANNOUNCEMENT TWO: THIS IS OUR TIME TO DRESS UP!!! Saturday night is going to be fun. Put on your best clothes, pull out that formal or semi-formal dress or suit, WHATEVER you want to wear. Maybe we will have time set aside for a GONG SHOW that night, maybe about 20 or 30 minutes, maybe that is where my talent lies. Almost forgot, approximately 15-20 minutes will be allocated for fashions from local stores.

ANNOUNCEMENT THREE: L. Hall and H. Hall are preparing a family history book in conjunction with R. Tate. If you have some information about our heritage, please get in contact with L. Hall.

ANNOUNCEMENT FOUR: In December, the Smith FAMILY GAZETTE will be published. At that time, a registration form will be included, this way I will have a good idea of the number of people who plan to come to the reunion. If you did not receive a personal copy of this information letter, please send your address to me so you can receive your copy of the newsletter (don't like the gazette part, maybe we will announce a contest to rename it). Smith FAMILY GAZETTE - got some news, did you find the love of your life (does he have a brother), win a contest, want to challenge a family in one of our numerous contests, got a new job, had a baby, left a job, lost weight, pregnant, finally learned how to cook, got new school clothes, SEND ANY TIDBIT TO ME BEFORE NOVEMBER 1, 1992. All of this information will be published in the first issue of the Smith Family Gazette, volume one, number one (other issues: March and May).

OTHER TIDBITS:

1. Packages, maps, places of worship, and restaurants and all other information will be available Thursday, the day of registration
2. Suggestion by family members: For family members to compile a recipe book, partial profits will be used to defray costs of reunion activities.
3. Suggested by Committee Chair: Educational Fund, rules and regulations to be discussed at a later date (also suggested that the name should be in memory of E. Smith.

OTHER NEWS:
Births
Illnesses
Deaths
Relocations
Promotions
Marriages
Engagements

APPENDIX D:

REGISTRATION FORM

Name_____

Address_____

_____

Telephone number_____

Descendent of_____

Talent for Show_____

Instrument_____

Comments_____.

Each day, envision

A GOAL!

PLAN,

have FAITH,

be DETERMINED,

WORK hard and long hours,

MAKE SACRIFICES -

ACHIEVE YOUR GOAL!

APPENDIX E

ALTERNATIVE REUNION LOCATIONS

After visiting many countries in Europe, someone asked me about a location in Georgia, my home state. I did not have an answer. It was then that I decided to discover my state and the wealth of opportunities for fun in my country. Some states are undiscovered territory. Many locations are beautiful and reasonable. Contact the Chamber of Commerce and Visitors' Bureau in any city for additional information (Numerous fun locations exist across the United States. The author has provided a sample from her visits. In no way does the author intend to infer that other valuable locations do not exist).

1. Cruise
   The top of my list is a cruise. The work is done for you. Make arrangements ahead of time with a cruise coordinator for your reunion. Your party shows up for days of planned pleasure.

2. Nevada
   Las Vegas offers a variety of package deals. Food is dirt cheap. Reno is another popular city.

3. Tennessee
   These cities guarantee fun for all: Nashville, Chattanooga, Memphis, and Knoxville. Nashville, immediately, country music comes to mind. Visit Nashville, you will be amazed by the variety of entertainment.

4. Georgia
   Does it appear that I am just a wee bit biased? Not really, Georgia is a beautiful and unusual state. Talk about going to another dimension! Each city listed is as different from the other according to its location, as night is to day. Yes, I have included more here on Georgia. I admit to being biased.

   Islands: St. Simon, Jekyll, Sea; Other locations: Savannah, Pine Mountain, Atlanta, Columbus, Helen, Augusta, Stone Mountain,

Brunswick, Albany, Rome, Athens

5. Louisiana
   New Orleans, need I say more; even kids will enjoy their visit.
   Shreveport, Bossier City, Baton Rouge,

6. Alabama
   Birmingham (hilly, beautiful and gracious); Mobile (fantastic);
   Eufaula (fishing anyone) is close enough to Dothan and
   Cottonwood (health resort) to select for a variety of fun for
   everyone. Other interesting cities: Montgomery, Selma, Tuscaloosa

7. Florida
   Select any city and you will discover fun. Try Jacksonville and head
   south for a tour

8. Mississippi
   Vicksburg, Jackson, and Bilouxi, are all unusual cities, especially if
   you are interested in civil war history. If not, these cities are close
   enough together to visit each while touring the state for your
   reunion. You will discover unusual treasures in each city.

9. Kentucky
   Louisville, Bowling Green, Cave City, Lexington
   Put this state somewhere on your list of reunion possibilities.

10. Indiana
    Indianapolis is close to many larger areas. Gary, a once popular
    mill town is close to Chicago. The city is small and offers many
    opportunities for enjoyable pleasure.

11. Virginia
    Select any city, I have visited several. Each location is unique and
    offers fun. I love this state! A lot of history is found in almost
    every city. Lots of sea food and shopping.

12. Washington, D.C.
    Our nation's capitol has had its share of bad events. However, you
    will miss a whole adventure if you overlook this city as a reunion

alternative. Opportunities for fun abound.

13. Delaware

Wilmington, so you have never dreamed of visiting Delaware? Visit, and discover a state that is centrally located with all kinds of adventure. Try a dinner cruise for me while you are there.

14. Massachusetts

Boston, sea food, great shopping, history. Just across the way is Cambridge. This state is a fantastic location for a reunion. Prices are reasonable.

15. Maryland

Baltimore offers many pleasant memories for your reunion. Plus, it is just a skip from so many unique cities.

16. South Carolina

Charleston is a city of pure, refined pleasure. Visit, you will discover the south at its finest.

17. Wisconsin

Milwaukee, and I am sure there are other equally unique cities to visit in Wisconsin. Start your reunion in this fantastic place and tour to other locations.

18. Illinois

Chicago is one of my favorite places to visit, but not during rush hour. The restaurants are so-o unusual. Yes, I do enjoy food. If it is jazz, a play, history, the arts in any form that you desire, Chicago is the place for your reunion.

19. Colorado

Denver (you think of skiing, I think of restaurants and tours), Colorado Springs, Boulder, Golden, City of the Gods. My family held a reunion in Colorado. The memories, we had fun!

20. Idaho

I was amazed by this state. When I hear the name, my mind automatically thinks of potatoes. But can you believe a wine is produced in Idaho? Skiing in Sun Valley is the absolute best.

21. Texas

Austin, Dallas/Ft. Worth, Houston, San Antonio, yes, Texas is a huge state with much to see. San Antonio can hold your attention for weeks. The combination of cultures in this city baffle the imagination. Each and every time I visit, I discover something unusual.

22. California

Such fun is waiting for you in California. Anaheim, San Diego, Los Angeles (forget television for a moment), San Francisco offer the best of any leisure activity for your family. Ladies visit the garment district in Los Angeles, talk about bargains.

23. Utah

Salt Lake City offers a variety of activities for your family. The city seems to be family oriented. Visit the Mormon Tabernacle Church and its library. Your family's history awaits you.

24. Pennsylvania

Philadelphia offers fun for all ages. Discover your family and our country's history at the same time. You will be glad that you added this state as a reunion location. Schedule a tour of the city and then drive to other equally interesting cities from this central location.

25. Ohio

Cincinnati, Cleveland, Columbus
When I visited sections of Cincinnati, I was at peace. This state is a treasure.

26. Michigan

Detroit, Lansing, Ypsilanti
Discover Michigan, oh so very close to Canada. So if you plan a reunion for these locations, you get pluses of both countries.

27. North Carolina

Charlotte, Greenville, Winston-Salem, Raleigh, Durham

North Carolina is a beautiful state with a variety of sceneries. Inland find rolling hills and on the coast find beautiful beaches.

28. West Virginia
    Charleston (only city I have visited)
    Hills you want, find them in West Virginia.

29. New York
    Rochester, Buffalo, Syracuse, Albany, New York City
    This state offers excitement, and it also offers a quiet atmosphere.
    New York has so many exciting places. Plus, it is close to Canada.

30. Virgin Islands
    This is it! Schedule a cruise or fly over. Go ANYWHERE, you are
    bound to have fun.

Now for places I have not visited long enough to give you an opinion. Some I have never visited. Each state offers exciting adventures.

Thinking about skiing during your family's winter time reunion. Try These locations and some listed above:

North Dakota, South Dakota, Montana, Rhode Island, Vermont, New Hampshire, Washington, Alaska, Maine, Iowa, Oregon (beautiful all year round), Alaska (try a spring or summer cruise), Nebraska, Minnesota

These locations have reasonable locations for family reunions:
New Mexico, Connecticut, Kansas, Missouri, New Mexico, Arizona, Hawaii, Wyoming, Puerto Rico, Canada (Americans are so close to Canadians not to venture and discover the opposite culture. Try it). Montreal, Quebec is a beautiful city with lots to see and do. Other Canadian locations: Toronto, Ottawa and London Ontario

APPENDIX F:
FAMILY INVENTORY

Name _____   Religious Affiliation_____

Address_____   Occupation_____

Telephone #(s)_____   Hobbies_____

Is it okay to contact you at work? Yes____ No____ #_____

Best time and day to call_____

Area of expertise_____

Projects in progress_____

Community activities_____

_____

Greatest accomplishments_____

_____

Awards_____

Strengths_____

_____

Interests_____

Aspirations_____

Summarize your experience in investments on the back.

Are you interested in increasing your present portfolio?

APPENDIX G:

PERSONAL HISTORY INFORMATION SHEET

<u>PART I</u>

Number on ancestry chart:_____

Name:_____

Nicknames and name changes_____

Address:_____

Born:_____   Place_____

Father's name_____

Mother's complete name_____

Religious affiliation_____

Clubs, lodges, societies_____

Occupation_____

Military service_____

<u>Schools attended</u> (start with elementary)_____

_____

_____

PART II

<u>Marital Status</u> (list all marriages and years, especially if

children were born)_____

_____

<u>Number of children</u> (Please indicate multiple births and

deceased children)

Child One: Name: Present age:

        Birth: Marriages:

        Death: Burial:

Child Two: Name   Present age:

        Birth: Marriages:

        Death: Burial:

Child Three:Name: Present age:

        Birth: Marriages:

        Death: Burial:

Child Four: Name: Present age:

        Birth: Marriages:

        Death: Burial:

<u>Include information on heirlooms and history on reverse side</u>

APPENDIX H

ANCESTOR CHART

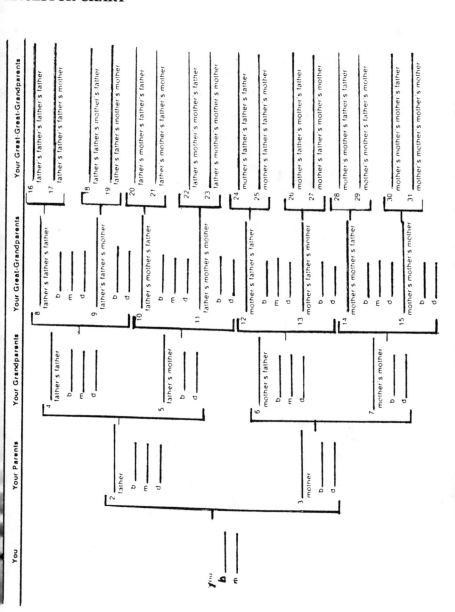

APPENDIX I

MAP OF THE UNITED STATES

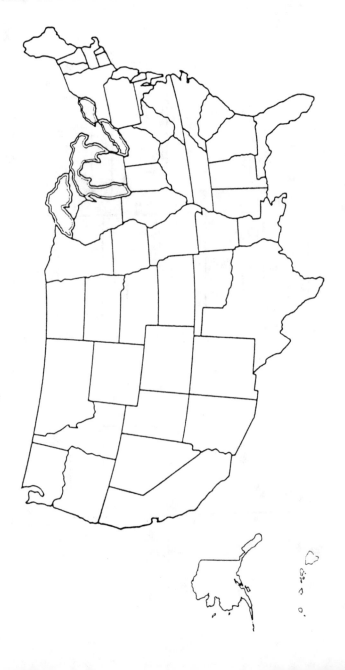

GLOSSARY

Ancestor chart - diagram of a family line starting with the present generation and going as far back in history as possible

Connect - to identify, facilitate, and maintain a family relationship

Discover - awareness of family relationships through seeking behavior

Family line - generations of relatives traced as descendants of one relative

Family of origin - birth family

Family unit - family residing together in one dwelling

Family Reference Guide - summary of pertinent family information distributed to all family members as a resource

Genealogy - scientific study of family history

Mutual fund - a method of investing money that is pooled with other investors (large and small) through an advisor for the benefits of volume purchasing.

No load - no fees attached to service when investing - rare.

Pedigree - detailing of genealogy in chart or other written form

Reunion - gathering of relatives for any period of time to renew family relationships and to discover others.

Thorned rose - symbolism for division of relatives within a family line according to characteristics of a thorned rose: delicate, strong, nurturing, and enigmatic.

Yield - money earned from investments

BIBLIOGRAPHY

Bossard, J.H. & Boll, E.S. (1976). *Ritual in family living: A contemporary study.* Westport, Connecticut: Greenwood Press Publishers.

Filby, P. W. (1970). *American and British Genealogy and Heraldry: A selected list of books.* Chicago: American Library Association.
compendium of books on genealogy

Peacock, V.S. (1980). *A family heritage workbook.* Missoula, MT: VSP Co.
a workbook, example of how to arrange your file system

Rawson, H. & Miner, M. (1986). *The new international dictionary of quotations.* New York: New American Library.

Redford, D.S. (1988). *Sommerset homecoming: Recovering a lost heritage.* New York: Doubleday.
example for writing your family's history

Stryker-Rodda, H. (1983). *How to climb your family tree: Genealogy for beginners.* Baltimore: Genealogical Publishing Co.
general information on family history and genealogy

Westin, J.E. (1977). *Finding your roots: How every American can trace his ancestors at home and abroad.* Los Angeles: The J.P. Tarcher, Inc.
general information on topic

INDEX

Exciting productions and presentations
by Dr. Turner

1. Fathers Cry, Too   (Book, audio tape set, training format)
2. It's Your Time To SOAR   (audio tape)
3. Starting A Home Business: Over 28 Tips That Save You Time and Money, third printing   (brochure with booklet to follow)
4. Mastering The Art of Public Speaking   (audio tape)
5. Change From Within: How To Achieve In Today's Society (book)
6. Family Reunions - Love 'Em!   (presentation)
7. Teaching Children and Adults About the Mythical Money Tree (book)

TO RECEIVE A CATALOG OF REUNION PRODUCTS (especially the "Thorned Rose Award") call or write to the following address:

Turner and Associates Consulting
  *Health and Respite Care
  MISSION SQUARE
  2901 Cody Road, Suite 12
  P. O. Box 6427; Columbus, GA 31902
  Columbus, Georgia 31907
(706) 569-7214 (Monday-Friday, 9am-5pm)

For Visa or Mastercard orders
call (706) 689-5121 7am to 5pm or fax after 5pm to 11pm

Are you interested in making a movie of your family's history with old photos? Contact Milton Turner of Milton's Creations for a free brochure. All transactions are completed by mail, fast and reliable. To order your movie call (205) 281-6991.

Geneva Turner is an international speaker with an abiding interest in family unity and family dynamics. She is an Associate Professor of nursing at Columbus College in Columbus, Georgia. Dr. Turner received nursing degrees from Columbus College, Georgia Southwestern, University of Alabama in Birmingham, and Texas Woman's University. While completing requirements for a doctorate, she obtained a minor in home and family living from the school of family science.

Dr. Turner is a family life educator certified by the National Association of Family Relations. She is available as a family reunion speaker. Other presentation topics are: grief experience of fathers, Alzheimer's Disease, the mythical money tree, plus others.

THORNED ROSE AWARD

A statue and a plaque are designed for presentation during family reunions. More information available July 1993. Call Family Projects Publishers/Turner and Associates Consulting Firm for a brochure.

ADVERTISING OPPORTUNITY

Do you have a title or product for sale? Advertise it in The Thorned Rose Catalogue. Advertising in a group catalogue is more feasible for the one or two product business owner, so is the advertising space. Send for space confirmation forms right away. Deadline is October 1, 1993.

REUNION TEE-SHIRTS AND OTHER REUNION GOODIES (REGISTRATION BAGS, HATS, CUPS, SUNGLASSES, GAMES, much more)

Do you need reunion tee-shirts and other items that enhance your reunion at a reasonable price? Some are available with your very own design? Contact F. P. P./ Turner and Associates, we can solve your problem with a fast turn around.

FUND RAISER!

Do you belong to an organization that is in need of operational funds or money for a project? Contact Family Projects Publishers/TACF for information on a fund raising activity that earns money with little effort for your group.